MAD

MADISON PUBLIC LIBRARY

P9-CPV-121

JAN 9 7 RECD

MARILYN
THE STORY OF A WOMAN

MADISON PUBLIC LIBRARY
MADISON, WISCONSIN

due Feb. 24 - 98

DATE DUE

DEMCO, INC.

IN MEMORY OF
MY FATHER,
LESLIE S. HYATT

COPYRIGHT © 1996 KATHRYN HYATT

A SEVEN STORIES PRESS FIRST EDITION

10 9 8 7 6 5 4 3 2 1

ALL RIGHTS RESERVED.

NO PART OF THIS BOOK MAY BE REPRODUCED, STORED IN A DATA BASE

OR OTHER RETRIEVAL SYSTEM, OR TRANSMITTED IN ANY FORM, BY ANY MEANS,

INCLUDING MECHANICAL, ELECTRONIC, PHOTOCOPYING, RECORDING OR OTHERWISE,

WITHOUT THE PRIOR WRITTEN PERMISSION OF THE PUBLISHER.

LIBRARY OF CONGRESS CATALOGING-IN-PUBLICATION DATA

HYATT, KATHRYN, 1950.

[GRAPHIC NOVEL. ENGLISH.]

—MARILYN: THE STORY OF A WOMAN.

1. MARILYN MONROE. 2. BIOGRAPHY—GRAPHIC NOVEL

I. KATHRYN HYATT

95-073164

CIP

PRINTED IN THE UNITED STATES

TABLE OF CONTENTS

MADISON PUBLIC LIBRARY

Mama's Girl

NEW YORK CITY 1955: MARILYN MONROE BEGINS HER STUDIES AT THE FAMOUS ACTOR'S STUDIO.

①

HELLO, I'M DR. KRIS.

DETERMINED TO BECOME A SERIOUS ACTRESS,

MARILYN ENTERS PSYCHOANALYSIS TO COME IN TOUCH WITH HER "EMOTIONAL MEMORY."

FOR A LONG TIME MY LIFE DIDN'T BELONG TO ME.

IF IT DIDN'T BELONG TO YOU, WHO DID IT BELONG TO THEN?

I DUNNO, MY MOTHER, I GUESS.

...AND ALL THOSE OTHERS.

TELL ME WHAT IT WAS LIKE WHEN YOU WERE A LITTLE GIRL.

SOME OF MY EARLIEST MEMORIES ARE OF CHURCH AND JESUS.

YES, JESUS LOVES ME...

YES, JESUS LOVES ME...

THE BIBLE TELLS ME SO...

NOT IN A PUBLIC RESTAURANT, NORMA JEANE.

THERE WAS A LITTLE PRINTING PRESS BEHIND THE KITCHEN.

I LEARNED THAT WHEN I WAS VERY BAD, I GOT THE RAZOR STROP,

WHEN I WAS A LITTLE BAD, I GOT ATTENTION.

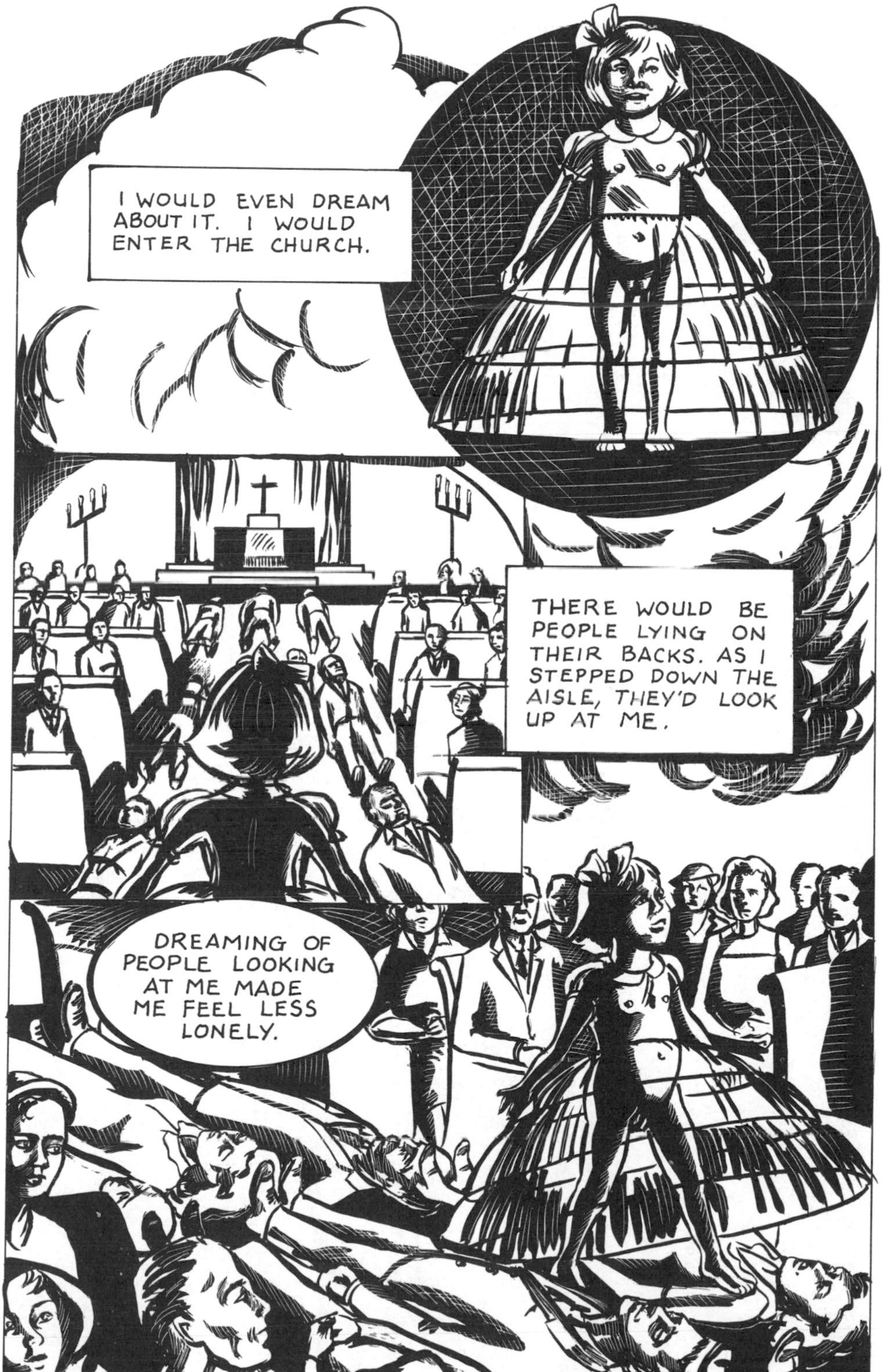
I WOULD EVEN DREAM ABOUT IT. I WOULD ENTER THE CHURCH.
THERE WOULD BE PEOPLE LYING ON THEIR BACKS. AS I STEPPED DOWN THE AISLE, THEY'D LOOK UP AT ME.
DREAMING OF PEOPLE LOOKING AT ME MADE ME FEEL LESS LONELY.

ONE NIGHT SOMETHING HAPPENED.

LOOK MOMMY!

MOMMY, DID YOU SEE ME SWIM?!

DON'T CALL ME "MOMMY."

CALL ME "AUNT."

BUT HE'S MY DADDY.

NO, NORMA JEANE.

WE ARE NOT YOUR PARENTS.

THE ONE WHO COMES HERE WITH THE RED HAIR. SHE'S YOUR MOTHER.

SO, I BELONG TO HER.

SHE NEVER SMILES.

ROOMS TO RENT

WHEN WE ARE ALONE, SHE SELDOM TALKS.

DON'T MAKE SO MUCH NOISE, NORMA JEANE.

THE ONLY TIME SHE SEEMS HAPPY IS WHEN SHE'S WITH A MAN.

BE ON YOUR GOOD BEHAVIOR, NORMA JEANE. HE MAY BE YOUR NEW DADDY.

SAY "CHEESE."

BUT MOST OF THE TIME SHE JUST FRIGHTENED ME. I SPENT A LOT OF TIME HIDING,

MY FAVORITE PLACE WAS AMONG THE CLOTHES IN HER CLOSET.

FOR A LONG TIME I SPENT MY WEEKENDS WITH MY MOTHER, THEN RETURNED TO MY AUNT & UNCLE.

AUNT IDA AND UNCLE WAYNE HAD A SON ABOUT MY AGE, LESTER.

WE SHARED A BEDROOM.

SOUNDS LIKE WHOOPING COUGH.

WAFF WAFF

SOON, I WAS SICK TOO.

NO GLADYS, THERE'S NOTHING ANYONE CAN DO TONIGHT.

THE DOCTOR SAYS THERE'S NO DANGER.

LET ME TALK TO HER.

REALLY IT'S NOT NECCESSARY... IDA AND I WORRY ABOUT YOU TRAVELING ACROSS TOWN IN THE MIDDLE OF THE NIGHT... WE PROMISE WE'LL LOOK AFTER HER.

THEY WERE TALKING TO MY MOTHER.

WHEN I WOKE UP, SHE WAS THERE.

SHE DIDN'T LEAVE.

I DON'T KNOW HOW LONG IT WENT ON,

IT FELT LIKE A LONG TIME.

WE'RE NOT ALWAYS GO-ING TO LIVE LIKE THIS, NORMA JEANE.

I'VE BEEN SAVING MY MONEY. SOMEDAY I'M GOING TO BUY US A HOUSE. THEN WE WILL ALWAYS BE TOGETHER.

I DIDN'T CRY WHEN SHE WENT BACK TO HER ROOMS, BACK TO HER JOB. I BE-LIEVED MY MOTHER.

A NEW FEELING WAS BEGINNING INSIDE ME.

LOOK WHAT FOLLOWED ME HOME FROM WORK.

IT WAS LIKE IT HAD ALWAYS BEEN THERE, JUST WAITING TO COME ALIVE.

YOU'VE BECOME VERY QUIET.

I WAS JUST THINKING.

I HAD ALL THIS FAITH, ALL THIS TRUST. HAPPINESS IS ALWAYS JUST AROUND THE CORNER, JUST OUT OF REACH.

THAT'S THE WAY MY LIFE HAS BEEN UP TO NOW.

DO YOU WANT TO BE HAPPY?

WELL YES! DOESN'T EVERYONE?

"LIFE, LIBERTY, AND THE PURSUIT OF HAPPINESS" THAT'S WHAT IT SAYS IN THE DECLARATION OF INDEPENDENCE.

YOU WERE LAUGHING, NOW YOU'VE BECOME QUIET AGAIN.

I WAS JUST REMEMBERING SOMETHING MY AUNT GRACE SAID...

DON'T MAKE YOUR MOTHER'S MISTAKE, NORMA JEANE. DON'T BREAK YOUR HEART CHASING IMPOSSIBLE DREAMS.

WAS AUNT GRACE YOUR MOTHER'S SISTER?

SHE WASN'T A REAL AUNT.

SHE WAS MY MOTHER'S BEST FRIEND AND MY LEGAL GUARDIAN FOR THE LONGEST TIME.

GIVE AUNT GRACE A KISS.

MY MOTHER USED TO BRING HER ALONG ON OUR SATURDAYS. SOMETIMES WE WENT TO GRAUMANS CHINESE THEATER OR THE AMBASSADOR HOTEL.

OH MY GOD!

IT'S MARY PICKFORD!

ISN'T SHE BEAUTIFUL?

DO YOU SEE THAT FUR?

THOSE MUST BE REAL DIAMONDS!

THAT WAS AMERICA'S SWEETHEART, THE MOST FAMOUS MOVIE STAR IN HOLLYWOOD.

SOMEDAY YOUR NORMA JEANE'S GOING TO BE A MOVIE STAR, I CAN FEEL IT IN MY BONES.

MY MOTHER AND AUNT GRACE WORKED TOGETHER AT COLUMBIA STUDIOS. AUNT GRACE WAS A FILM LIBRARIAN AND MY MOTHER WAS A FILM CUTTER. SOMETIMES MY MOTHER TOOK ME TO WORK WITH HER...

AT WORK MY MOTHER WAS LIKE ANOTHER WOMAN. PEOPLE SEEMED TO LIKE HER.

SHE WAS SO PRETTY. I GUESS I WAS VERY PROUD OF HER.

I THOUGHT THIS WAS ALL GOING TO BE PART OF OUR NEW LIFE... THIS NEW, HAPPIER MOTHER WOULD GO ALONG WITH OUR NEW HOUSE.

IF MY MOTHER WAS AS NERVOUS AND WITHDRAWN AS EVER WHEN WE WERE ALONE, I TRIED NOT TO NOTICE.

THIS WAS ONE OF THE HAPPY TIMES.

LOOK!

HE WAVED AT US!

IT TURNS OUT THAT THE AVIATOR WAS A FRIEND OF MY MOTHER.

I WAS STILL LIVING WITH MY "AUNT + UNCLE."

...BLESS MAMA, AUNT IDA UNCLE WAYNE, LESTER AND TIPPY TOO.

TIPPY SLEPT WITH ME.

THRATCH THRATCH

SHUSH! TIPPY! WE'LL BOTH GET A PADDLING.

THRATCH THRATCH

WHAT IF I GIVE YOU SOME FOOD? IS THAT WHAT YOU WANT?

BARK BARK BARK

HERE TIPPY, PLEASE EAT, PLEASE.

OK, I'LL LET YOU OUT, BUT PLEASE BE CAREFUL.

WHEN I FINALLY FELL ASLEEP, I DREAMED I WAS IN A PLANE WITH MOTHER + TIPPY.

WE WERE DOING LOOP-DE-LOOPS

THE ARCS WERE GETTING WILDER AND WILDER...

PEOPLE WERE APPLAUDING ON THE GROUND.

...THEN I SAW MYSELF AND TIPPY AMONG THE PEOPLE ON THE GROUND.

HA HA HA WE'RE CRASHING

BANG SHREEE...

NEXT MORNING I HEARD THE MILKMAN TALKING TO MY UNCLE.

SORRY, BUT THE LITTLE FELLA HAS COURTED HIS LAST LADY.

I HEARD MY UNCLE TALKING TO MY AUNT.

DON'T TELL NORMA JEANE.

I STAYED WAY BEHIND WHEN I FOLLOWED MY UNCLE TO AN EMPTY LOT.

HE STOPPED AND JUST STOOD THERE.

TIPPY. HIS EYES WERE OPEN. BUT THERE WAS BLOOD IN HIS MOUTH.

FROM THEN ON THINGS TOOK A TURN.

THERE WAS AN EARTHQUAKE. WE SLEPT OUTSIDE A FEW NIGHTS FOR FEAR THE HOUSE WOULD FALL DOWN ON US.

SWEET JESUS, BE WITH US TONIGHT, PROTECT US...

PLEASE JESUS TAKE CARE OF TIPPY. HE REALLY WASN'T A BAD DOG. IT WAS MY FAULT...

IT STILL HURTS.

YEAH, AFTER ALL THESE YEARS.

THAT TIME MY MOTHER CAME AND NURSED ME...

... AND TIPPY.

RING

THUMP THUMP

THOSE WERE THE ONLY TIMES I FELT SPECIAL.

IT GAVE ME HOPE THAT GOOD THINGS COULD HAPPEN TO ME.

I THOUGHT I COULD BE LIKE OTHER KIDS.

THEN LATER IT ALL BECAME LIKE SOME KIND OF CRUEL JOKE.

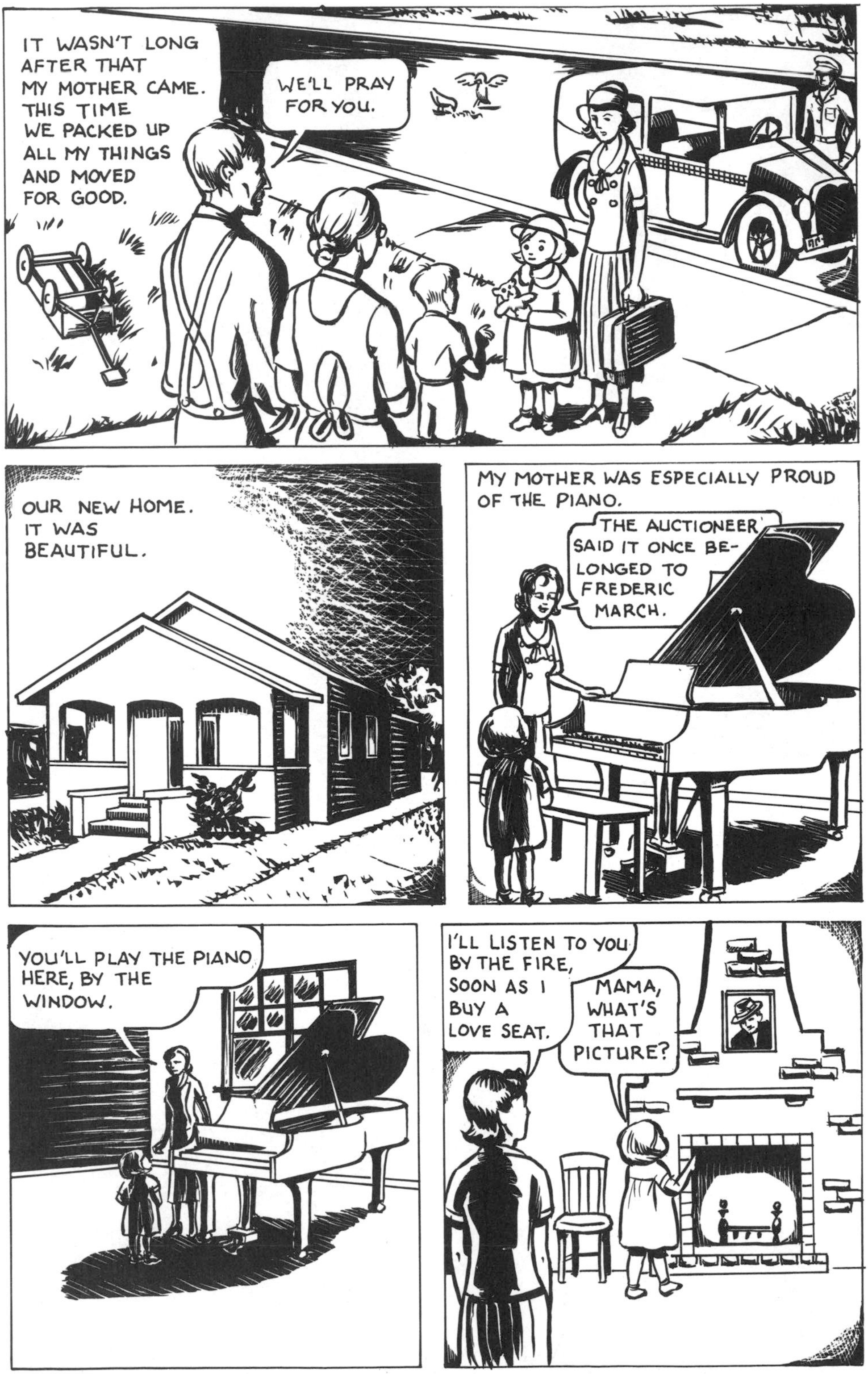
IT WASN'T LONG AFTER THAT MY MOTHER CAME. THIS TIME WE PACKED UP ALL MY THINGS AND MOVED FOR GOOD.
WE'LL PRAY FOR YOU.
OUR NEW HOME. IT WAS BEAUTIFUL.
MY MOTHER WAS ESPECIALLY PROUD OF THE PIANO.
THE AUCTIONEER SAID IT ONCE BE-LONGED TO FREDERIC MARCH.
YOU'LL PLAY THE PIANO HERE, BY THE WINDOW.
I'LL LISTEN TO YOU BY THE FIRE, SOON AS I BUY A LOVE SEAT.
MAMA, WHAT'S THAT PICTURE?

HERE, STAND ON THIS CHAIR AND GET A GOOD LOOK.

THAT'S YOUR FATHER.

I WAS SO EXCITED I ALMOST FELL OFF THE CHAIR.

HE DIED IN A CAR ACCIDENT IN NEW YORK.

I DIDN'T BELIEVE IT, IT WAS SO GOOD TO FIND MY FATHER. I COULDN'T LOOSE HIM.

WHAT'S HIS NAME, MAMA?

SHE WOULDN'T ANSWER. SHE JUST WENT INTO THE BEDROOM AND LOCKED THE DOOR.

THIS WAS THE DEPRESSION, WE KEPT MY BEDROOM AND MY MOTHER'S. WE RENTED OUT THE REST OF THE HOUSE TO A FAMILY OF ENGLISH ACTORS.

HELLO, DUCKIE.

PING

THE FATHER WAS THE STAND-IN FOR THE ACTOR, GEORGE ARLISS.

THE MOTHER DID WALK-ON PARTS IN COSTUME PICTURES.

THE DAUGHTER WAS SO PRETTY, SHE BECAME MADELINE CARROLL'S STAND-IN.

IT WAS REALLY THE ENGLISH FAMILY THAT INTRODUCED ME TO THE MOVIES. ON SATURDAYS THEY'D TAKE ME TO GRAUMAN'S CHINESE OR EGYPTIAN.

I'D BE THERE BY MYSELF ALL DAY, WATCHING MOVIES OVER AND OVER I'D WALK HOME BY MYSELF, SOMETIMES AFTER DARK.

I DIDN'T MIND. I LOVED IT.

I HAD MY FAVORITES, CLAUDETTE COLBERT, JEAN HARLOW, AND ESPECIALLY CLARK GABLE.

CLARK GABLE LOOKED SO MUCH LIKE THE PHOTO OF MY FATHER, I PRETENDED HE WAS MY FATHER.

COMING ATTRACTION

THE FUNNY THING ABOUT THIS ARRANGEMENT IS THAT I DIDN'T SEE MUCH MORE OF MY MOTHER THAN WHEN I LIVED WITH AUNT IDA AND UNCLE WAYNE. SHE WAS ALWAYS WORKING.

SHE WOULD COME HOME LATE AT NIGHT.

SATURDAY USED TO BE 'OUR DAY'. NOW SHE WORKED ON SATURDAYS TOO.

MY MOTHER STILL HAD MEN FRIENDS, BUT NEVER ANYONE FOR TOO LONG.

THIS LASTED ABOUT THREE MONTHS.

YOUR MUM'S GOT ONE OF HER HEADACHES TODAY, SO DON'T DAWDLE.

I WAS GETTING USED TO MY MOTHER, THE ENGLISH FAMILY...

'BYE MAMA, I'M GOING.

... THE NEW SCHOOL AND ALL.

I DIDN'T UNDERSTAND THEN, I FOUND OUT MUCH LATER...

MY MOTHER CALLED IN SICK THAT DAY,

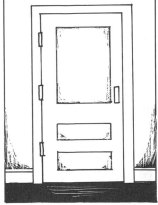

THEY SAY SHE WENT INTO THE KITCHEN FOR MORE COFFEE.

CRASH
HA HA HA

SMASH

I SUPPOSE MY MOTHER DIDN'T WANT MUCH.

SHE WANTED A HUSBAND AND HOUSE FOR US TO LIVE IN.

YOU'D BETTER COME, GRACE.

SHE JUST WANTED TO BE HAPPY.

CALM DOWN GLADYS, IT'S ME.

I KNOW WHO YOU ARE.

YOU WANT TO POISON ME!

I'VE BEEN CUT!

MY MOTHER ENDED UP IN NORWALK STATE HOSPITAL.

SHE LIVES IN AN INSTITUTION TO THIS DAY.

I CONTINUED LIVING IN THAT HOUSE WITH THE ENGLISH PEOPLE.

THEN THEY SOLD THE FURNITURE TO PAY THE MORTAGE.

THE ACTOR GEORGE ARLISS RETURNED TO ENGLAND & SO DID HIS STAND-IN.

STIFF UPPER LIP, LUV.

AUNT GRACE LOST HER JOB AT COLUMBIA.

DAY-OLD BREAD 25¢ A SACK FULL

IT WAS A MATTER OF TIME BEFORE I WAS SENT TO THE ORPHANAGE.

...WHERE OLD DREAMS DIE AND NEW DREAMS COME ALIVE.

IT HURT MY HEART TO DREAM OF BEING LOVED AND WANTED AS OTHER CHILDREN.

THE ONLY DREAM LEFT WAS TO BE BEAUTIFUL, TO BE NOTICED.

NOW IT'S FUNNY TO HEAR PEOPLE SAY I'M BEAUTIFUL.

SOMETIMES I DON'T FEEL BEAUTIFUL INSIDE.

WHY AREN'T YOU ASLEEP NORMA JEANE?

SOMETIMES I DON'T FEEL VERY BEAUTIFUL AT ALL.

BY THE TIME I WAS TWENTY
I HAD FOUND SOME SUCCESS WORKING
AS A MODEL AND PIN-UP GIRL,
ENOUGH SUCCESS TO BE NOTICED
BY A MOVIE STUDIO.

I SIGNED A CONTRACT WITH
TWENTIETH CENTURY FOX.
A YEAR LATER — WITH A
NEW NAME AND ONE
PERFORMANCE ON THE
CUTTING ROOM FLOOR
I WAS DISMISSED
FOR BEING
"UNPHOTOGENIC."

IN A TOWN FULL OF
BEAUTIFUL STARLETS
ASPIRING TO BE THE
NEXT BETTY GRABLE
OR RITA HAYWORTH,
I WAS ——.

The Girl Least Likely to Succeed

②

THE ACTOR'S LAB

HAIL TO THEE BLITHE SPIRIT,
SWEET BIRD THAT THY WIRTH...

VERY GOOD,
EXCELLENT PROJECTION,
... NOW MISS MONROE.

GULP

HAIL TO THEE
BLITHE
SQUEAK

MISS MONROE, I'D LIKE TO SPEAK TO YOU BEFORE YOU LEAVE...

DEAR, I WANT TO GIVE YOU SOME ADVICE, AND I WANT YOU TO TAKE IT IN THE SPIRIT IT IS GIVEN.

I'M AFRAID YOU'RE WASTING YOUR TIME AND MONEY ON ACTING LESSONS

OH NO!

YOU'RE VERY DILIGENT VERY HARD WORKING BUT IN SOME CASES THAT ISN'T ENOUGH.

I KNOW I'LL GET BETTER!

OH DEAR, YOU'RE NOT GOING TO MAKE THIS EASY...

YOUR WORK IS VERY SELF-CONSCIOUS, YOUR VOICE IS VERY SMALL, LITTLE MORE THAN A SQUEAK.

YOU DON'T HAVE THE POISE OR SELF-POSSESSION YOU NEED TO BECOME AN ACTRESS.

NOW, NOW, I'M REALLY FOND OF YOU. I KNOW YOU'RE STRUGGLING... PERHAPS YOU COULD FIND A JOB.

SNIFF.

I APPLIED AT KRESKE'S ONCE, BUT THEY DIDN'T HIRE ME BECAUSE I DIDN'T GRADUATE FROM HIGH SCHOOL.

YOU'RE A VERY PRETTY GIRL, THERE MUST BE SOMEONE SPECIAL.

NO.

PLEASE GIVE ME ANOTHER CHANCE! THE MONEY ISN'T IMPORTANT!

BECOMING AN ACTRESS IS EVERYTHING TO ME...

OH, ALRIGHT.

I JUST DON'T WANT TO GIVE YOU FALSE HOPE.

THANK-YOU! SOMEDAY YOU'LL BE PROUD OF ME, YOU'LL SEE.

SCHWAB'S DRUGSTORE—HEADQUARTERS FOR ASPIRING STARS AND STARLETS.

MY AGENT DOESN'T DO A THING FOR ME. IF ONLY...

HIRED HER ON THE SPOT—SHE WASN'T EVEN TRYING TO BREAK INTO THE BUSINESS. SHE WAS JUST VISITING HER BROTHER.

OF ALL THE DUMB LUCK.

HEY MARILYN, WHAT WILL IT BE TODAY? A NICE JUICY HAMBURGER?

DON'T BE A COMEDIAN. I'LL HAVE MY USUAL.

ONE BOTTOMLESS CUP OF COFFEE COMING UP.

MARILYN I'M GLAD YOU CAME.

HI, SID.

JOE SCHENCK'S * BEEN TRYING TO CALL YOU.

YOU KNOW WHO SHE IS? SHE'S OLD MAN SCHENCK'S GIRL!

NO!

TELEPHONE

* JOE SCHENCK, RETIRED CO-FOUNDER OF TWENTIETH CENTURY FOX.

WELL, IT DIDN'T DO HER MUCH GOOD, FOX DROPPED HER ANYWAY.

WANT TO KNOW THE REAL REASON FOX DROPPED HER?

THEY SAY SHE WAS VERY, VERY CLOSE TO ZANUCK'S* FORMER FUTURE SON-IN LAW.

NOW HE'S A GROOM WITHOUT A BRIDE...

...AND SHE'S A STARLET WITHOUT A STUDIO.

*DARYL ZANUCK, STUDIO HEAD AND CO-FOUNDER OF TWENTIETH CENTURY FOX.

HA HA HA HA HA

SO WHO ARE THEY LAUGHING AT?

ANY GOOD NEWS?

I GUESS HE NEEDS AN ORNAMENT FOR HIS DINNER PARTY. WELL, I CAN ALWAYS USE A GOOD MEAL.

WHEN I WENT INTO THE BUSINESS, ONE OF THE FIRST THINGS I DID WAS BUY THE LOUDEST, LOWEST CUT RED DRESS I COULD FIND...

I HATED TO DO IT IN A WAY, BUT I HAD A LONG WAY TO GO AND I NEEDED A LOT OF NOTICING.

AFTER DINNER

HOW ARE THINGS GOING, MARILYN?

ABOUT THE SAME. I JUST MAKE THE ROUNDS TO ALL THE AGENCIES AND CASTING OFFICES.

LAST WEEK, I GOT A COUPLE NIGHTS WORK WHEN A MAGICIAN'S ASSISTANT GOT SICK.

YOU WERE VERY QUIET TONIGHT, ANYTHING WRONG?

MY ACTING INSTRUCTER SAYS I DON'T HAVE THE TALENT AND POISE TO BECOME AN ACTRESS.

WHAT DO YOU THINK?

I KNOW I'M NOT VERY GOOD.

BUT I CAN LEARN, I HAVE TO . . .

THERE'S MORE TO BEING A SUCCESS IN THIS TOWN THAN BEING AN "ACTRESS."

YOU WANT TO BE A SUCCESS, DON'T YOU?

WELL YES, BUT...

GOOD! TRY COLUMBIA

THERE MIGHT BE SOMETHING THERE.

YES, MISS MONROE.

WE'VE BEEN LOOKING FOR AN ACTRESS OF JUST YOUR TYPE.

I MUST BE DREAMING!

JUST A FEW FORMS TO FILL OUT,

CASTING OFFICE

HE MUST SEE HUNDREDS OF GIRLS...

... BEAUTIES OF ALL SORTS.

AND YOU'LL BE ON THE PAYROLL.

MAYBE HE SEES SOMETHING SPECIAL IN ME.

YOU OUGHT TO GO FAR HERE.

BUT WHY ME?

THE FIRST PEOPLE I THOUGHT OF WERE AUNT GRACE AND AUNT ANA.

WHEN I GET MY FIRST PAY-CHECK I'LL BUY AUNT GRACE A BOTTLE OF PERFUME.

WON'T SHE FEEL ELEGANT!

THIS MATCHING BED JACKET AND SLIPPERS WILL MAKE AUNT ANA FEEL LIKE A QUEEN.

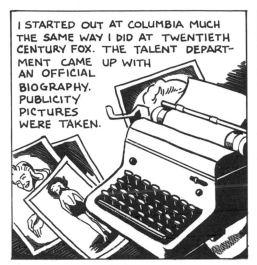

I STARTED OUT AT COLUMBIA MUCH THE SAME WAY I DID AT TWENTIETH CENTURY FOX. THE TALENT DEPARTMENT CAME UP WITH AN OFFICIAL BIOGRAPHY. PUBLICITY PICTURES WERE TAKEN.

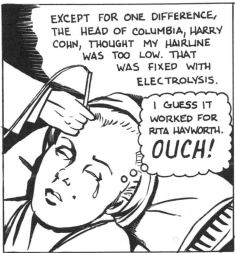

EXCEPT FOR ONE DIFFERENCE, THE HEAD OF COLUMBIA, HARRY COHN, THOUGHT MY HAIRLINE WAS TOO LOW. THAT WAS FIXED WITH ELECTROLYSIS.

I GUESS IT WORKED FOR RITA HAYWORTH. **OUCH!**

THE STUDIO PROVIDED VOCAL COACHING WITH MR. FRED KARGER...

♪ LOVE ME ♪ OR LEAVE ME

GOOD PITCH, NOW PROJECT!

... AND ACTING LESSONS WITH MISS NATASHA LYTESS.

HAIL TO THEE, BLITHE SPIRIT...

BREATHE, MISS MONROE!

I HAD A CONTRACT WITH A STUDIO. MY DREAMS WERE COMING BACK IN BRIGHT, SHINY COLORS, SCARLET, GOLD AND BLUE...

RING RING

MARILYN, TELEPHONE.

I'M AFRAID I HAVE BAD NEWS, DEAR.

IT WAS AUNT GRACE.

AUNT ANA HAS PASSED AWAY.

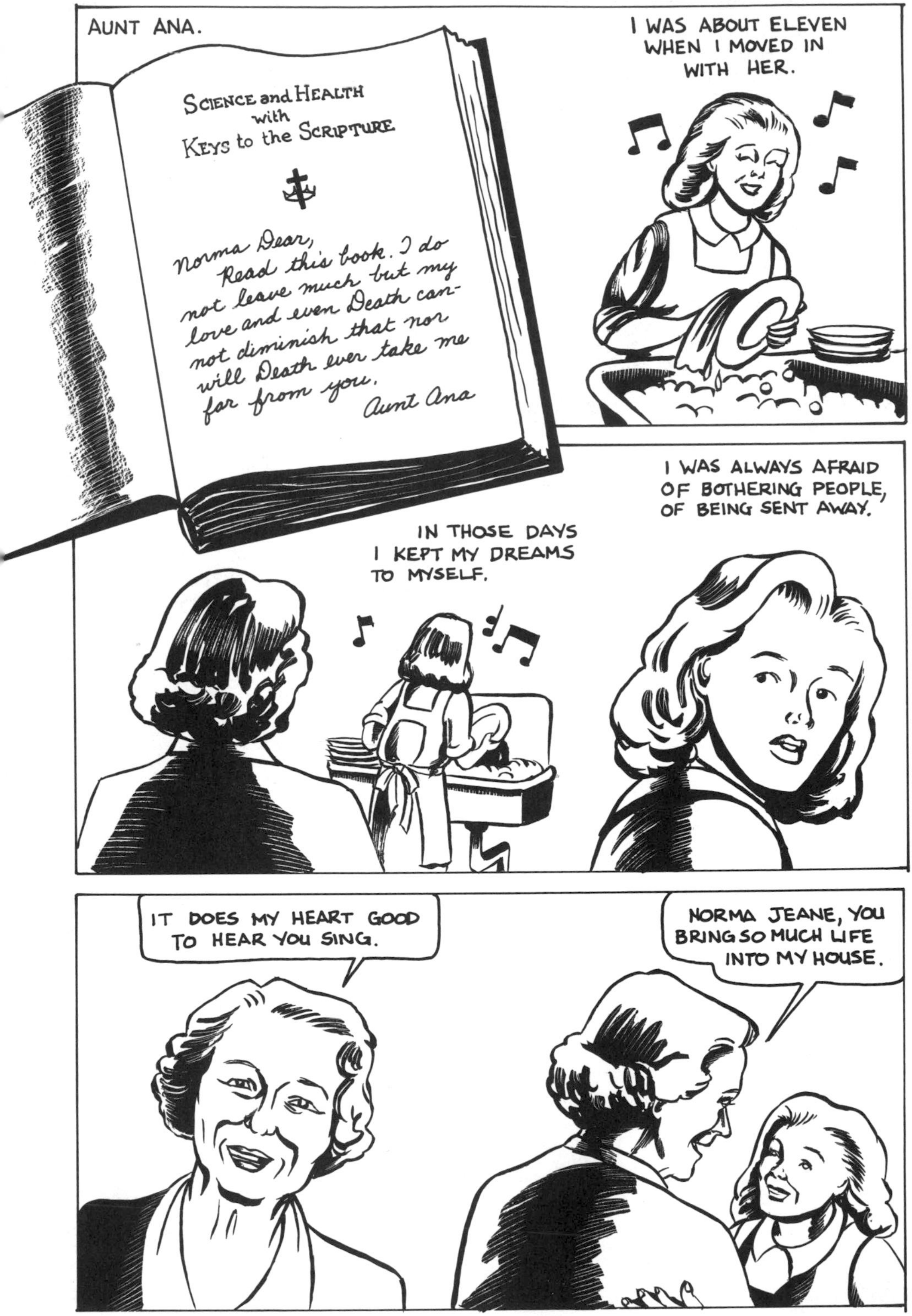
AUNT ANA.
SCIENCE and HEALTH with KEYS to the SCRIPTURE
Norma Dear, Read this book. I do not leave much but my love and even Death cannot diminish that nor will Death ever take me far from you. Aunt Ana
I WAS ABOUT ELEVEN WHEN I MOVED IN WITH HER.
I WAS ALWAYS AFRAID OF BOTHERING PEOPLE, OF BEING SENT AWAY.
IN THOSE DAYS I KEPT MY DREAMS TO MYSELF.
IT DOES MY HEART GOOD TO HEAR YOU SING.
NORMA JEANE, YOU BRING SO MUCH LIFE INTO MY HOUSE.

WHAT GOOD IS A MOVIE CONTRACT? WHAT GOOD IS ANYTHING WITHOUT AUNT ANA?

I WENT BACK TO THE PLACE WHERE SHE LIVED...

I HAD TO TALK TO SOMEONE. BUT ANA WAS THE ONLY ONE. I HAD... I WANTED TO END THIS HORRIBLE ACHE,

I WANTED TO SEE THE LAST THING ANA SAW.

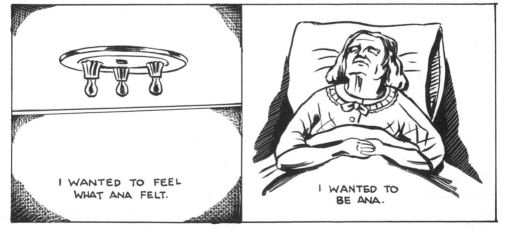

I WANTED TO FEEL WHAT ANA FELT.

I WANTED TO BE ANA.

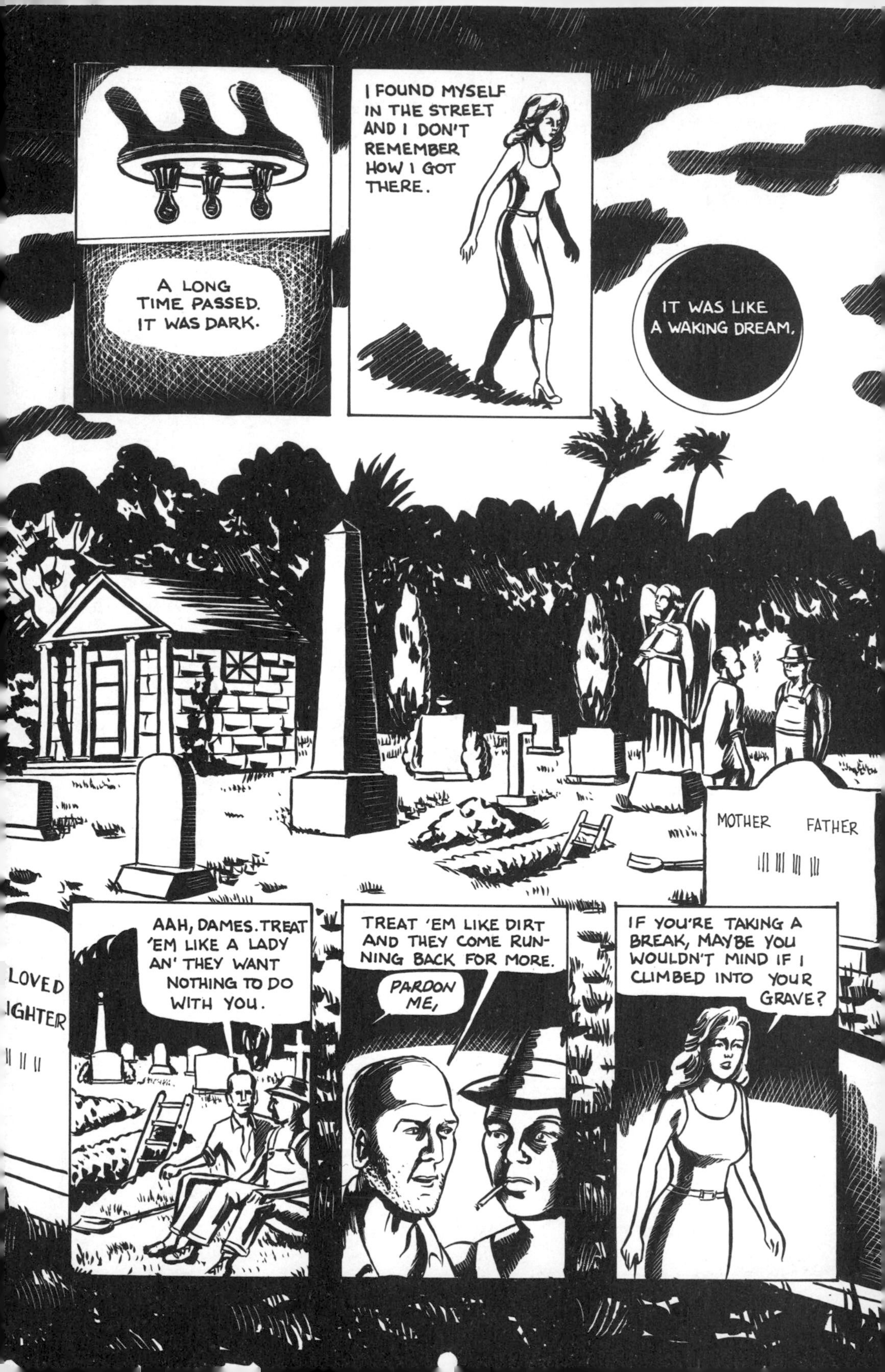

A LONG TIME PASSED. IT WAS DARK.
I FOUND MYSELF IN THE STREET AND I DON'T REMEMBER HOW I GOT THERE.
IT WAS LIKE A WAKING DREAM.
MOTHER
FATHER
LOVED
IGHTER
AAH, DAMES. TREAT 'EM LIKE A LADY AN' THEY WANT NOTHING TO DO WITH YOU.
TREAT 'EM LIKE DIRT AND THEY COME RUN-NING BACK FOR MORE.
PARDON ME,
IF YOU'RE TAKING A BREAK, MAYBE YOU WOULDN'T MIND IF I CLIMBED INTO YOUR GRAVE?

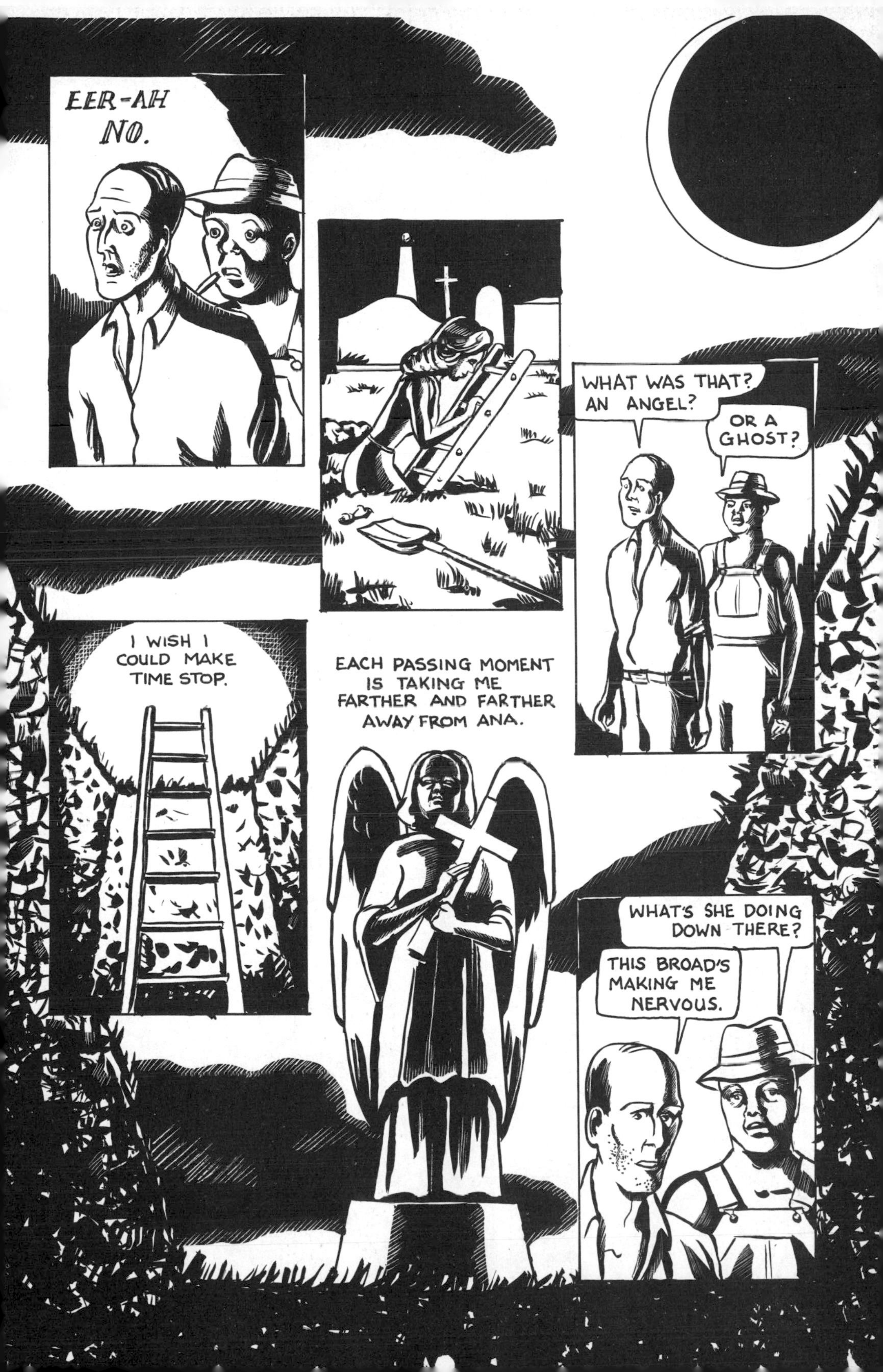
EER-AH
NO.
WHAT WAS THAT? AN ANGEL?
OR A GHOST?
I WISH I COULD MAKE TIME STOP.
EACH PASSING MOMENT IS TAKING ME FARTHER AND FARTHER AWAY FROM ANA.
WHAT'S SHE DOING DOWN THERE?
THIS BROAD'S MAKING ME NERVOUS.

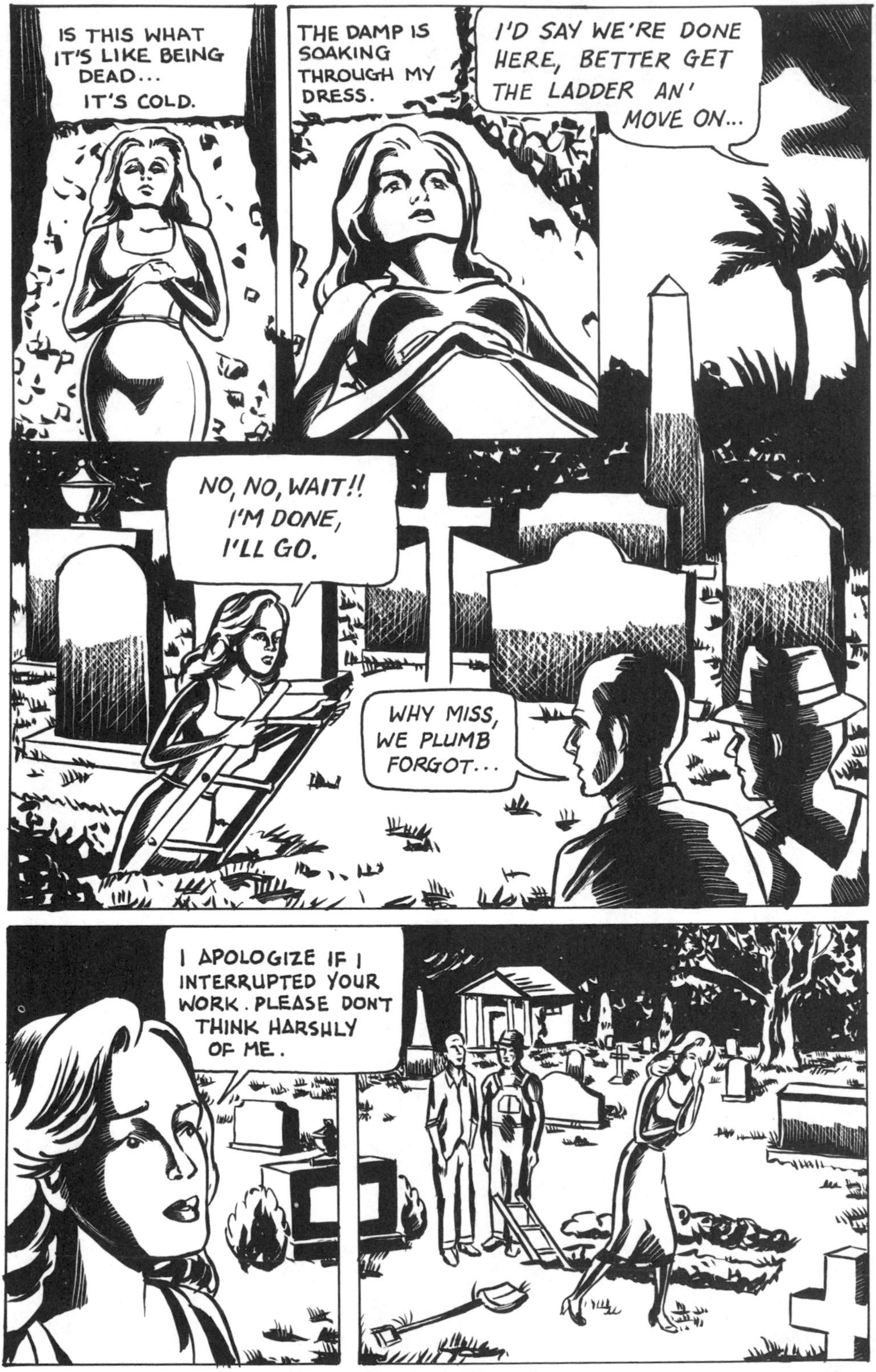
IS THIS WHAT IT'S LIKE BEING DEAD... IT'S COLD.
THE DAMP IS SOAKING THROUGH MY DRESS.
I'D SAY WE'RE DONE HERE, BETTER GET THE LADDER AN' MOVE ON...
NO, NO, WAIT!! I'M DONE, I'LL GO.
WHY MISS, WE PLUMB FORGOT...
I APOLOGIZE IF I INTERRUPTED YOUR WORK. PLEASE DON'T THINK HARSHLY OF ME.

IN SPITE OF EVERYTHING I WENT TO MY ACTING CLASS NEXT DAY. I HAD WORKED SO HARD TO GET THIS FAR, EVEN THOUGH IT WASN'T VERY FAR AT ALL.

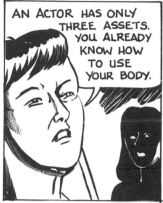

AN ACTOR HAS ONLY THREE ASSETS. YOU ALREADY KNOW HOW TO USE YOUR BODY.

BUT WHEN ARE YOU GOING TO LEARN TO USE YOUR VOICE?

WHEN ARE YOU GOING TO LEARN TO USE YOUR INTELLECT, MISS MONROE?

DRAMATIC ARTS DEPARTME

WELCOME

NEXT TIME YOU COME HERE BE PREPARED TO USE ALL YOUR ASSETS!

SLAM

YOU LOOK LIKE ANOTHER ONE OF NATASHA'S VICTIMS.

OH HI, SIDNEY.✷

✷SIDNEY SKOLSKY, COLUMNIST & MARILYN'S MENTOR.

WHY DOES SHE KEEP ME AS A STUDENT IF I'M SO TALENTLESS?

DON'T TAKE IT SO HARD. SHE'S LIKE THAT WITH EVERYONE.

AND THE WAY SHE KEEPS STARING AT ME! SHE'S SO INTENSE! I CAN'T IMAGINE WHAT'S GOING ON IN HER MIND.

YOU'VE GOT TO UNDERSTAND HER.

IN EUROPE SHE WAS AN ACTRESS, THEN CAME THE WAR AND SHE FOUND HERSELF IN HOLLYWOOD COMPETING WITH EVERY GLAMOUR GIRL LIKE YOU. SHE'S FRUSTRATED!

THE STUDIO KEPT ME BUSY AS "BACKGROUND" IN A FEW FILMS.

MARILYN MONROE.

JUNE HAVER.

NATALIE WOOD.

ALTHOUGH I DIDN'T APPEAR PERSONALLY, MY PHOTOGRAPH WAS A PROP IN A GENE AUTRY FILM, *RIDERS OF THE WHISTLING PINES.*

SWEET NELL, WHY DID YOU HAVE TO DIE?

MONTHS PASSED... I THOUGHT THE CASTING DIRECTOR HAD FORGOTTEN ME WHEN HE CALLED.

THERE'S A PART I WANT YOU TO AUDITION FOR... YOU'LL HAVE TO SING.

I WENT TO MY SINGING COACH, FRED KARGER.

I HAVE TO DO WELL AT THIS AUDITION, BUT FRED I GET SO NERVOUS.

DON'T WORRY, YOU'RE READY.

I'VE NEVER SUNG IN FRONT OF A LIVE AUDIENCE.

I CAN HELP YOU THERE.

THAT NIGHT FRED TOOK ME TO A HOUSE IN THE CANYON.

THINK OF MY FRIENDS AS YOUR FRIENDS, NO ONE WANTS TO SEE YOU FAIL.

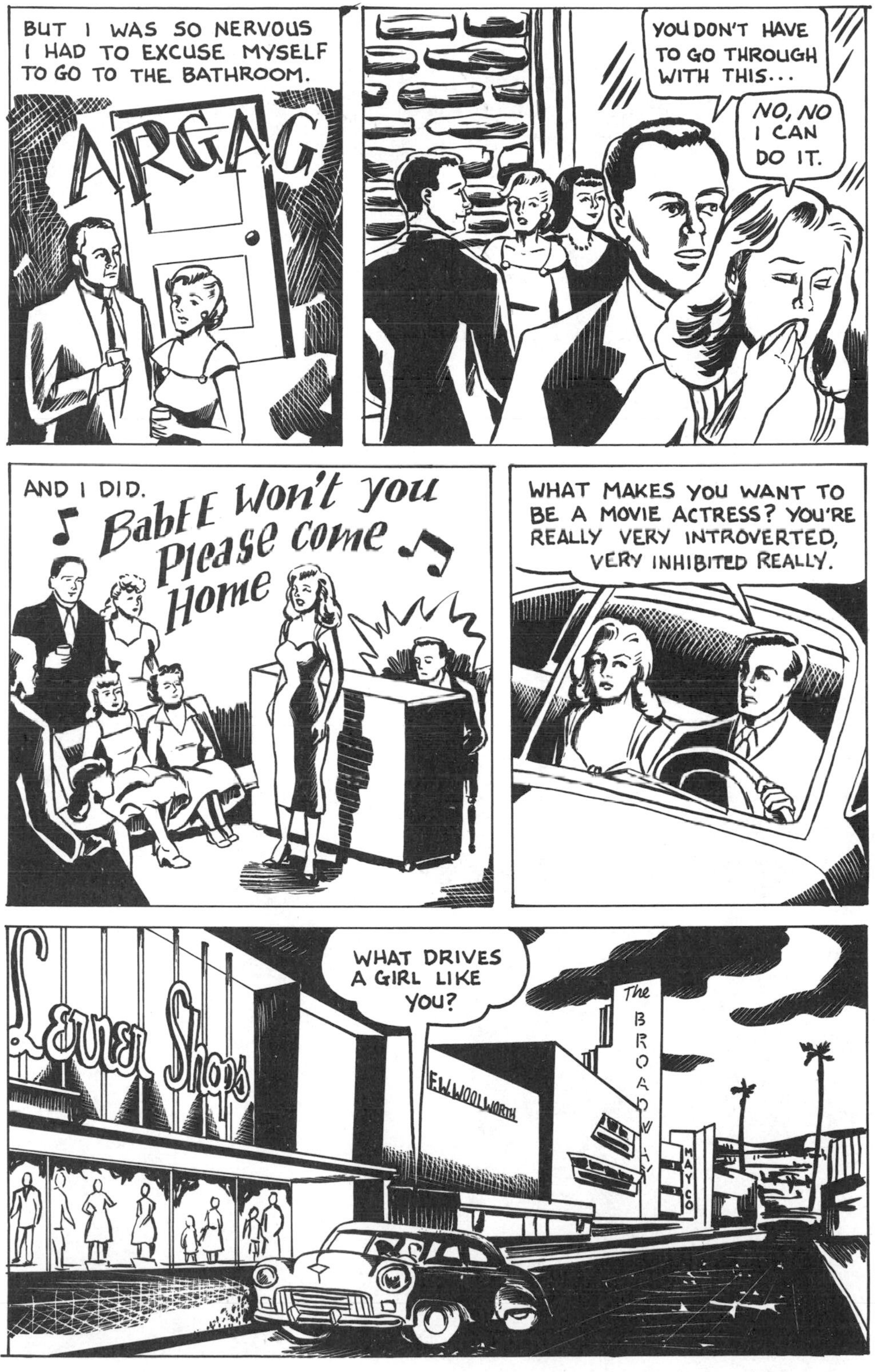
BUT I WAS SO NERVOUS I HAD TO EXCUSE MYSELF TO GO TO THE BATHROOM.
ARGAG
YOU DON'T HAVE TO GO THROUGH WITH THIS...
NO, NO I CAN DO IT.
AND I DID.
BabEE Won't you Please come Home
WHAT MAKES YOU WANT TO BE A MOVIE ACTRESS? YOU'RE REALLY VERY INTROVERTED, VERY INHIBITED REALLY.
Lerner Shops
WHAT DRIVES A GIRL LIKE YOU?
F.W. WOOLWORTH
The BROADWAY
MAY CO

I'VE ALWAYS KNOWN I WANTED TO BE AN ACTRESS, SINCE I WAS LITTLE.

SO DO LOTS OF GIRLS,

BUT MOST GIVE UP, SOONER OR LATER.

NOT ME.

THIS IS THE ONLY THING IN MY LIFE I CAN CONTROL.

OH I KNOW IT MAY NOT SEEM LIKE IT, NOT AFTER TONIGHT.

BUT THINGS HAVE BEEN WORSE FOR ME, FAR WORSE.

WHEN I WAS A KID I WAS HELPLESS TO DO ANYTHING ABOUT IT.

BUT NOT NOW, NOT ANYMORE.

Every BabEEE Needs a Da-Da DaddEEE

I AUDITIONED IN FRONT OF THE STUDIO HEAD, HARRY COHN. I WAS TERRIFIED BUT I GOT THE PART.

NOW THAT I HAD A ROLE IN A FILM I WAS BUSIER THAN EVER... AND I WAS SEEING MORE AND MORE OF FRED.

AT THAT TIME MOST OF THE MEN I MET HAD ONLY ONE THING ON THEIR MIND.

NONE OF THOSE MEN CARED IF I WAS SICK OR AFRAID.

FRED WAS STRONG AND KIND.

HE WAS EVERYTHING I DREAMED OF IN A MAN.

I THOUGHT HE WAS THE MAN I WAS GOING TO MARRY.

I WAS WORKING HARD, LEARNING MY TWO SONGS, PRACTICING MY DANCE ROUTINES...

AND STUDYING MY LINES.

MAMA, HE'S NOT LIKE DADDY. HE'S DIFFERENT.

GOOD, MUCH BETTER.

I ADMIT I DIDN'T SEE MUCH POTENTIAL IN YOU, BUT YOU'RE REALLY IMPROVING.

THANK-YOU, NATASHA.

THAT MEANS A LOT COMING FROM YOU, YOU'RE SUCH A CULTURED WOMAN.

THERE IS SO MUCH I WANT TO LEARN.

DID YOU READ THE BOOK I LENT TO YOU?

YES. CHEKHOV REALLY UNDERSTOOD PEOPLE, DIDN'T HE?

CHEKHOV

CHERRY ORCHARD

SEAGULL

UNCLE VANYA

HE WAS A PERSON OF GREAT HUMANITY.

CHEKHOV EMBODIES THE RUSSIAN SOUL!

CHEKHOV IS ONE OF THE GREAT MODERN DRAMATISTS.

MY RELATIONSHIP WITH MISS NATASHA LYTESS HAD GREATLY IMPROVED.

WHEN THE TIME CAME TO FILM *LADIES OF THE CHORUS* I ARRIVED EARLY AT THE SOUND-STAGE EACH DAY.

I HAD REHEARSED AND MEMORIZED MY LINES WORD PERFECT.

STILLS FROM *LADIES OF THE CHORUS*

IT WAS ONLY A "B" MOVIE, BUT YOU NEVER KNOW.

YOU HAVE TO TREAT EVERYTHING SERIOUSLY, AS IF THIS WERE YOUR BIG BREAK.

ONE DAY I GOT A CALL FROM MR. COHN'S SECRETARY.

BE AT MR. COHN'S OFFICE AT 4 O'CLOCK.

I WONDER WHY MR. COHN WANTS TO SEE ME?

HE MUST HAVE SEEN RUSHES OF MY FILM. MAYBE HE WANTS TO CAST ME IN ANOTHER PRODUCTION!

GET A HOLD OF YOUR-SELF, MARILYN, DON'T ACT TOO EAGER, DON'T GRIN LIKE AN IDIOT.

BE COMPOSED BE SELF-POSSESSED.

MR. COHN WILL BE RIGHT OUT.

COME INTO MY OFFICE, MISS MONROE.

TURN AROUND, LET'S GET A LOOK AT YOU.

VERY NICE, NICELY PUT TOGETHER.

I UNDERSTAND YOU STARTED OUT AS A PIN-UP GIRL.

YES, THAT'S RIGHT.

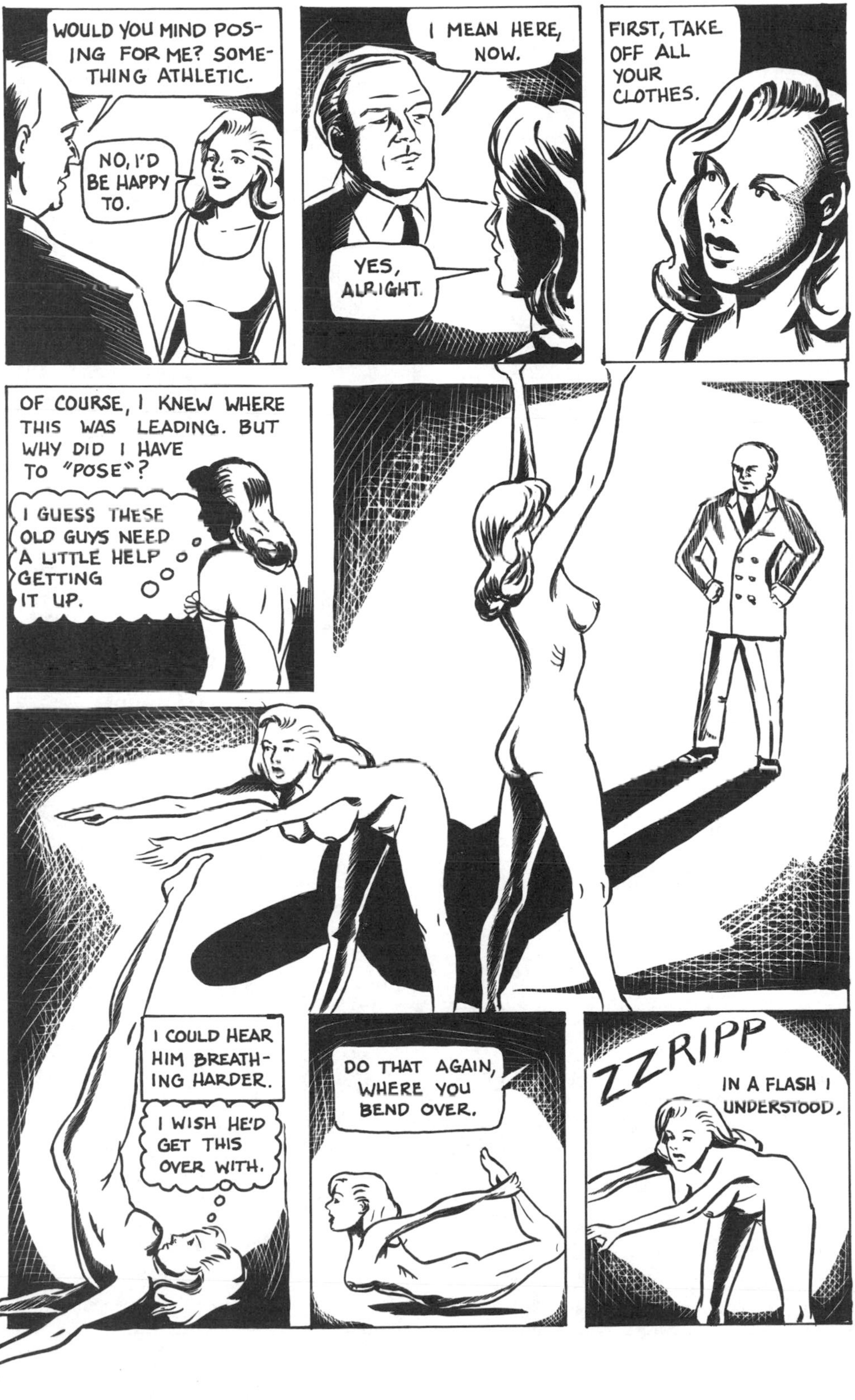
WOULD YOU MIND POSING FOR ME? SOMETHING ATHLETIC.
NO, I'D BE HAPPY TO.
I MEAN HERE, NOW.
YES, ALRIGHT.
FIRST, TAKE OFF ALL YOUR CLOTHES.
OF COURSE, I KNEW WHERE THIS WAS LEADING. BUT WHY DID I HAVE TO "POSE"?
I GUESS THESE OLD GUYS NEED A LITTLE HELP GETTING IT UP.
I COULD HEAR HIM BREATHING HARDER.
I WISH HE'D GET THIS OVER WITH.
DO THAT AGAIN, WHERE YOU BEND OVER.
ZZRIPP
IN A FLASH I UNDERSTOOD.

WAIT A MINUTE, I DON'T DO THIS.

WHAT'S WRONG WITH YOU?

YOU WANT TO *BUTT FUCK* ME. YOU WANT TO HURT ME.

SO?! IT CAN'T BE WORSE THAN SUCKING JOE'S DICK.

DON'T LOOK SO SHOCKED, I KNOW WHO YOU ARE.

YOU'RE JOE SCHENCK'S GIRL. HE TOLD ME ALL ABOUT YOU.

HE ASKED ME TO DO HIM A FAVOR AND GIVE YOU A JOB.

FACE IT, JOE'S TIRED OF YOU. HE WANTS TO GET RID OF YOU.

I COULD REALLY DO THINGS FOR YOU, IF YOU'RE NICE TO ME.

SLAP

WHY ARE SOME MEN SO SICK?

DOES IT MAKE THEM FEEL BIG TO HURT ME?

DO THEY LIKE TO HEAR ME BEG THEM TO STOP?

I WENT INSIDE A CHURCH. IT WAS ALL I COULD THINK TO DO. I FELT SO DIRTY.

I THOUGHT MR. SCHENCK WAS MY FRIEND. HOW COULD HE HAVE SAID THOSE THINGS? DOES HE REALLY THINK I CAN BE PASSED AROUND?

I'VE BEEN REJECTED BY ONE STUDIO. NOW MAYBE THIS ONE TOO.

MAYBE I AM AN UN-PHOTOGENIC, UN-TALENTED NOBODY.

WHY CAN'T I JUST GET A JOB?

I'M NOT AFRAID OF WORK.

LOTS OF GIRLS ARE HAPPY TO BE WAITRESSES OR CLERKS.

I'VE BEEN WASHING DISHES...

AND SCRUBBING FLOORS...

ALL MY LIFE.

NO, NO, I CAN'T DO THAT.

I CAN'T GO BACK TO THE DRAB WORLD OF NORMA JEANE, I JUST CAN'T.

SIX MONTHS AFTER I SIGNED WITH COLUMBIA MY OPTION FOR RENEWAL WAS DROPPED.

AFTER BEING DROPPED BY COLUMBIA, IT WAS BACK TO THE LIFE OF A FREELANCER.

WHEN HE SAYS "I HEAR AN OWL IN THE PINES", THAT'S MY CUE.

CRUNCH

OH MY GOODNESS! ARE YOU HURT?

DR. STEIN D.D.S.

I'M SO SORRY. IT'S MY FAULT, I WAS THINKING ABOUT MY AUDITION.

MY CAR HAS A LITTLE DENT, BUT IT'S NOT TOO BAD.

MY CAR'S LEAKING.

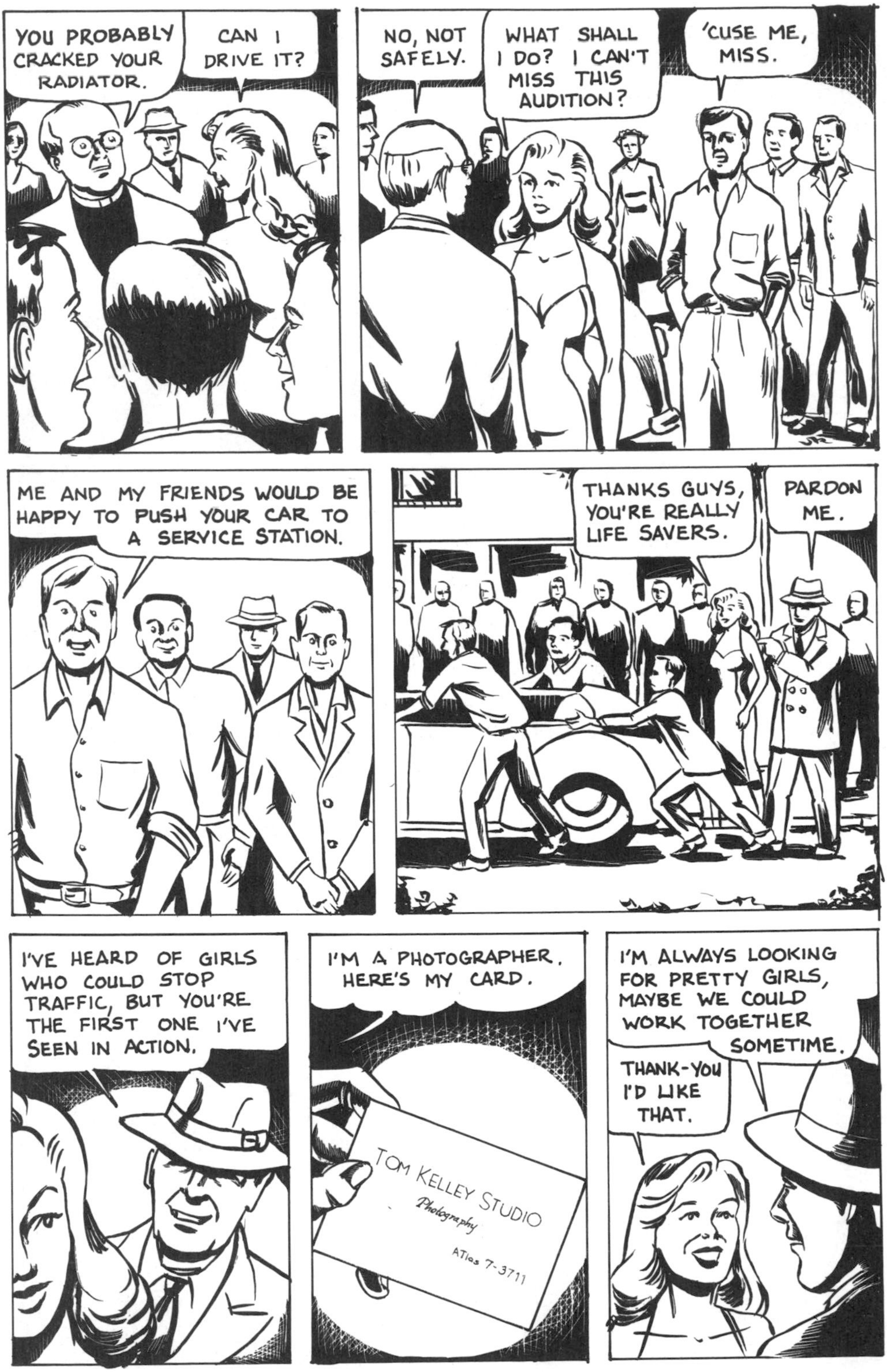
YOU PROBABLY CRACKED YOUR RADIATOR.
CAN I DRIVE IT?
NO, NOT SAFELY.
WHAT SHALL I DO? I CAN'T MISS THIS AUDITION?
'CUSE ME, MISS.
ME AND MY FRIENDS WOULD BE HAPPY TO PUSH YOUR CAR TO A SERVICE STATION.
THANKS GUYS, YOU'RE REALLY LIFE SAVERS.
PARDON ME.
I'VE HEARD OF GIRLS WHO COULD STOP TRAFFIC, BUT YOU'RE THE FIRST ONE I'VE SEEN IN ACTION.
I'M A PHOTOGRAPHER. HERE'S MY CARD.
TOM KELLEY STUDIO
Photography
ATlas 7-3711
I'M ALWAYS LOOKING FOR PRETTY GIRLS, MAYBE WE COULD WORK TOGETHER SOMETIME.
THANK-YOU I'D LIKE THAT.

I KEPT LOOKING FOR WORK, ALTHOUGH I WASN'T THINKING SO MUCH ABOUT "SUCCESS" ANYMORE.

MAYBE I SHOULD REVIVE MY MODELING CONTACTS.

THE USUAL.

WHO WAS THAT MAN, THE ONE WHO SAID I COULD STOP TRAFFIC? TOM KELLEY?

I HOPE I HAVEN'T LOST HIS CARD.

—BESIDES, I REALLY NEED A JOB.

HI SWEETIE, YOU BUSY TOMORROW?

NO, WHY?

THE MARX BROTHERS ARE SHOOTING RE-TAKES OF THEIR MOVIE.

THEY HAVE A LITTLE BIT FOR A SHAPELY BLONDE, SO NATURALLY I THOUGHT OF YOU.

SIDNEY, YOU DOLL.

NEXT MORNING I MET THE PRODUCER, GROUCHO AND HARPO MARX.

CAN YOU WALK?

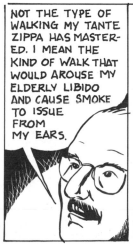

NOT THE TYPE OF WALKING MY TANTE ZIPPA HAS MASTER-ED. I MEAN THE KIND OF WALK THAT WOULD AROUSE MY ELDERLY LIBIDO AND CAUSE SMOKE TO ISSUE FROM MY EARS.

EXCEEDINGLY WELL DONE!

HONK HONK

AMAZING! SHE'S LIKE MAE WEST, THEDA BARA AND BO PEEP ROLLED INTO ONE.

WE SHOOT FIRST THING TOMORROW.

AND DON'T DO ANY WALKING IN UNPOLICED AREAS.

MR. GRUNION, I WANT YOU TO HELP ME.

WHAT SEEMS TO BE THE TROUBLE?

SOME MEN ARE FOLLOWING ME.

REALLY? I CAN'T UNDERSTAND WHY?

I WAS ON SCREEN LESS THAN 1 MINUTE IN *LOVE HAPPY*.

THE PRODUCER WAS VERY ENTHUSIASTIC ABOUT ME. I GOT A MENTION IN LOUELLA PARSON'S COLUMN AND SPECIAL BILLING IN THE CREDITS.

Introducing Marilyn Monroe

ONE DAY I MET HIM IN HIS OFFICE.

AFTER THE MOVIE IS RELEASED I WANT YOU TO GO ON A PROMOTIONAL TOUR.

YOU'LL GO TO NEW YORK, CHICAGO, ALL OVER THE MIDWEST. HOW DOES THAT SOUND?

WONDERFUL!

A MONTH AFTER COLUMBIA DROPPED ME, **LADIES OF THE CHORUS** WAS RELEASED.

THERE WASN'T ANY BIG HOLLYWOOD OPENING.

I SAW IT AT A NEIGHBORHOOD THEATER WITH FRED.

I RECEIVED MY FIRST REVIEW.

One of the brightest spots is Miss Monroe's singing. She is pretty and with her pleasing voice and style shows promise.
-Tibor Krekes
Motion Picture

MOST THINGS DIDN'T GO SO SMOOTHLY. MY ROMANCE WITH FRED WAS SOURING.

I LOVE YOU FRED, I'VE NEVER FELT LIKE THIS BEFORE.

YOU WILL AGAIN.

I DON'T KNOW I JUST KNOW YOU'RE EVERYTHING TO ME.

YOU SHOULDN'T BE SO EMOTIONAL.

WHAT'S MOST IMPORTANT IN LIFE TO YOU?

YOU ARE!

AND AFTER I'M GONE?

PLEASE DON'T EVEN TALK ABOUT THAT.

YOU CRY TOO EASILY. YOU NEVER THINK ABOUT LIFE.

YOUR MIND ISN'T DEVELOPED. COMPARED TO YOUR BREASTS, ITS EMBRYONIC.

WHY DOES HE TALK TO ME LIKE THAT?

I ARRANGED TO CONTINUE MY STUDIES WITH NATASHA. MORE THAN A TEACHER, SHE HAD BECOME MY FRIEND AND CONFIDANT.

FRED TREATS YOU LIKE A CONVENIENCE. HE ONLY SEES YOU WHEN THE MOOD STRIKES HIM.

I KNOW HE LIKES TO BE WITH ME.

I CAN TELL HE'S HAPPY TO SEE ME, HE SMILES ALL THE TIME WHEN WE'RE TOGETHER.

HE LIKES TO KID AND TEASE ME. I DON'T EVEN MIND WHEN HE CRITICIZES MY MIND.

YOU DON'T MEAN THAT!

A LOT OF WHAT HE SAYS IS TRUE! I DON'T KNOW MUCH ABOUT LIFE!

BUT I'M WILLING TO CHANGE. I'D DO ANYTHING FOR HIM!

YOU'RE SO INVOLVED YOU CAN'T SEE THE OBVIOUS.

HE DOESN'T LOVE YOU! LET HIM GO!

I CAN'T.

MARILYN, LET ME LOVE YOU.

DON'T LOVE ME, TEACH ME, NATASHA.

I HAD ALWAYS WONDERED WHY NATASHA STARED AT ME — BUT I NEVER GUESSED HOW SHE FELT.

NATASHA WAS RIGHT. HE CAN'T LOVE ME IF HE THINKS I'M SO FAR BENEATH HIM.

I GUESS I KNEW IT WAS ENDING. THAT'S WHY I'VE BEEN FEELING SO SAD.

RRIING RRIING

IT'S OVER. I MAY AS WELL FACE IT. IT'S OVER.

MARILYN PHOONE!

HELLO MARILYN! I HAVE A CLIENT, A CALENDAR MANUFACTURER INTRESTED IN YOU.

IT WAS TOM KELLEY, THE PHOTOGRAPHER

HE WANTS TO KNOW IF YOU'D CONSIDER POSING IN THE NUDE.

WELL, I DON'T KNOW.

I'VE POSED IN THE NUDE BEFORE, BUT THAT WAS FOR A PAINTER.

I PROMISE YOU IT WOULD BE VERY ARTISTIC, VERY TASTEFUL.

I HAVE MY MOVIE CAREER TO CONSIDER. IT WOULDN'T BE GOOD PUBLICITY.

I DON'T NEED AN ANSWER RIGHT AWAY.

PROMISE ME YOU'LL THINK ABOUT IT. IT PAYS $50.

OH, ALRIGHT. I'LL THINK ABOUT IT.

WOULDN'T FRED HATE IT IF I POSED NUDE? HMMP,

IT WAS BACK TO SKIPPING MEALS AND SCROUNGING FOR JOBS.

NOT MUCH EVER CAME OF IT, BUT I HAD TO KEEP MAKING THE ROUNDS.

MY CAR IS GONE!

I CALLED THE SHERRIF'S OFFICE.

MISS MONROE, YOUR CAR WASN'T STOLEN, IT WAS REPOSSESSED.

H09-2340

KILROY WAS HERE

I VISITED THE FINANCE OFFICE.

I NEED MY CAR. I CAN'T GET WORK WITHOUT IT.

UPON RECEIPT OF $50, WE WOULD BE HAPPY TO RETURN YOUR CAR.

BUT I DON'T HAVE $50.

I'M SORRY THEN, THERE'S NOTHING I CAN DO TO HELP.

I WENT BACK TO MY ROOM THINKING ALL THE WAY.

I ALMOST CALLED SOME BIG SHOTS I KNOW— BUT I WAS STOPPED BY THIS HOT ANGER INSIDE ME

THEN I ACTED LIKE I WAS TRYING TO BREAK OUT OF SOMEWHERE.

CRACK THUCK

HEY! WHAT'S GOING ON IN THERE?

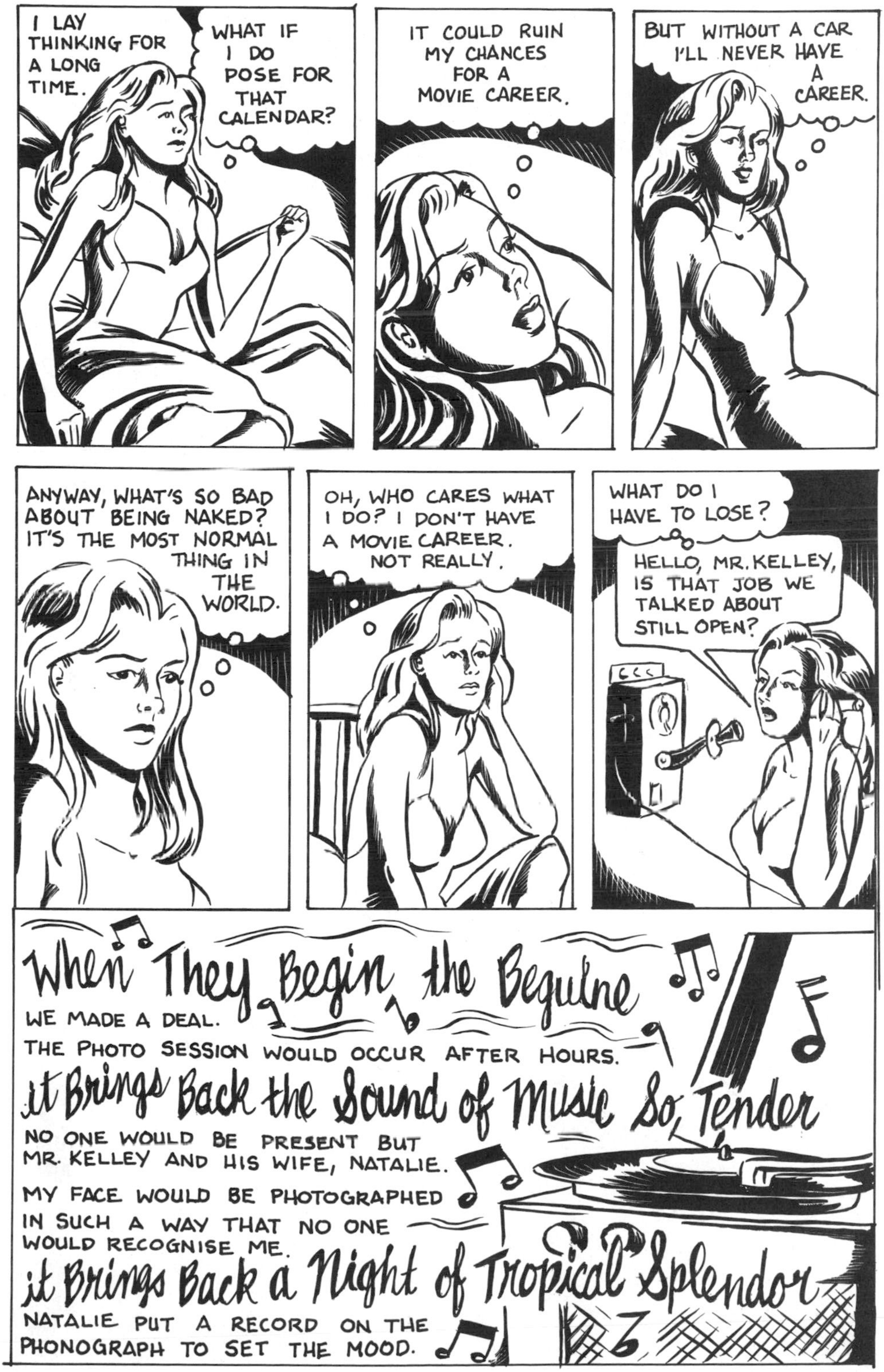
I LAY THINKING FOR A LONG TIME.
WHAT IF I DO POSE FOR THAT CALENDAR?
IT COULD RUIN MY CHANCES FOR A MOVIE CAREER.
BUT WITHOUT A CAR I'LL NEVER HAVE A CAREER.
ANYWAY, WHAT'S SO BAD ABOUT BEING NAKED? IT'S THE MOST NORMAL THING IN THE WORLD.
OH, WHO CARES WHAT I DO? I DON'T HAVE A MOVIE CAREER. NOT REALLY.
WHAT DO I HAVE TO LOSE?
HELLO, MR. KELLEY, IS THAT JOB WE TALKED ABOUT STILL OPEN?
When They Begin the Beguine
WE MADE A DEAL.
THE PHOTO SESSION WOULD OCCUR AFTER HOURS.
it Brings Back the Sound of Music So Tender
NO ONE WOULD BE PRESENT BUT MR. KELLEY AND HIS WIFE, NATALIE.
MY FACE WOULD BE PHOTOGRAPHED IN SUCH A WAY THAT NO ONE WOULD RECOGNISE ME.
it Brings Back a Night of Tropical Splendor
NATALIE PUT A RECORD ON THE PHONOGRAPH TO SET THE MOOD.

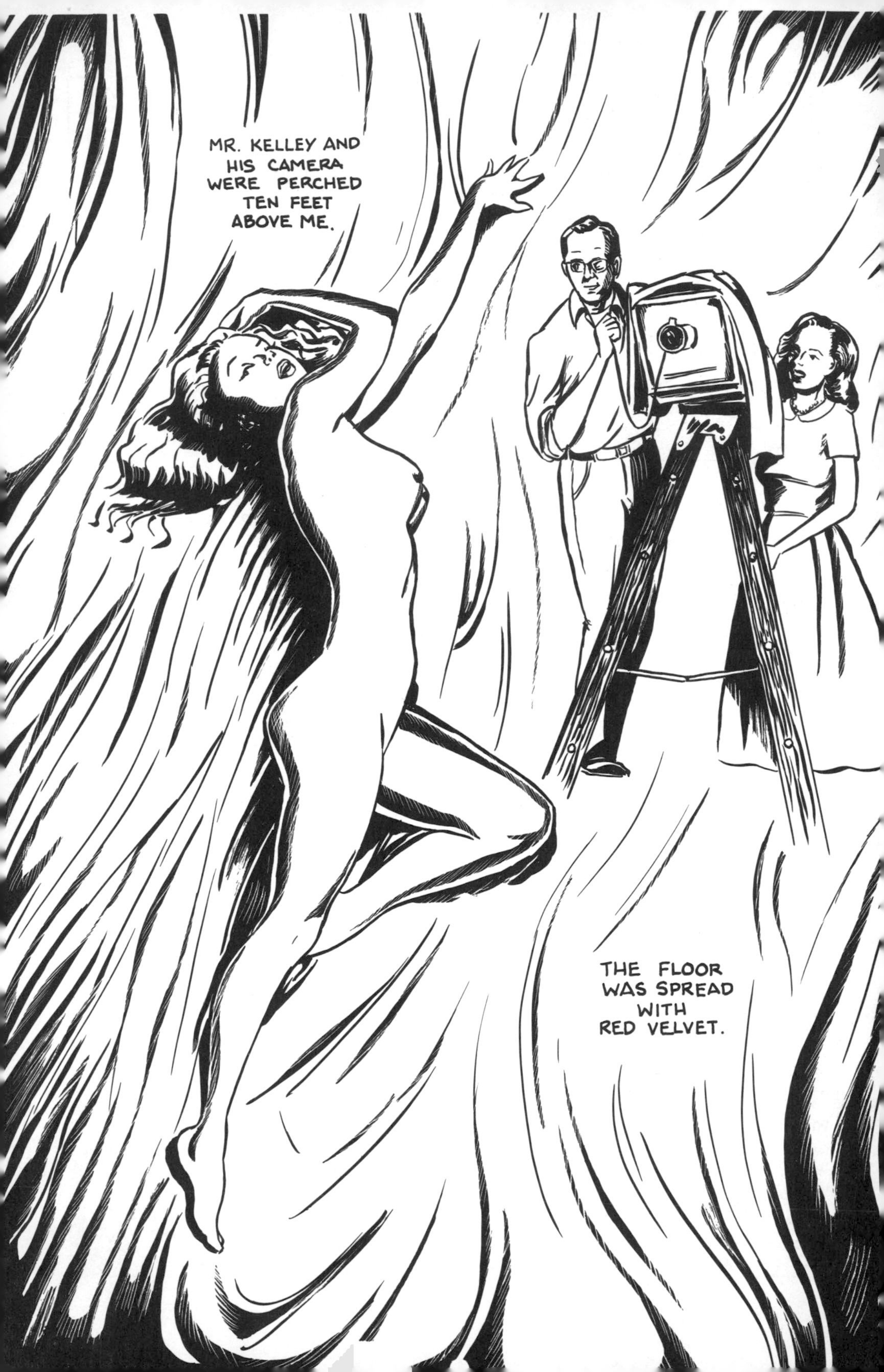
MR. KELLEY AND HIS CAMERA WERE PERCHED TEN FEET ABOVE ME.
THE FLOOR WAS SPREAD WITH RED VELVET.

AFTERWARD WE WENT TO BARNEY'S BEANERY FOR CHILI AND COFFEE.

MARILYN, I DON'T KNOW WHAT YOU DO IN FRONT OF THE CAMERA, BUT SOMETHING SPECIAL HAPPENS.

WHEN I WAS NEW IN THE BUSINESS MY HEART LEAP-ED EVERYTIME SOMEONE SAID I WAS "SPECIAL".

SINCE THEN I'VE HAD TOO MANY TROUBLES TO REALLY BELIEVE IT.

I KNOW IT'S TOUGH.

BUT YOU REALLY DO HAVE SOMETHING! WE SEE HUNDREDS OF GIRLS WHO DON'T.

THEN WHY CAN'T I GET ANYWHERE?

NO MATTER HOW HARD I WORK THINGS NEVER GET BETTER.

YOUR LUCK WILL CHANGE!

IT MAY TAKE YEARS, BUT IT WILL GET BETTER! I HAVE A FEELING ABOUT YOU!

AFTER THE BUSINESS WITH THE CAR I MOVED IN WITH NATASHA TO SAVE MONEY.

ONCE FRED STOPPED ME ON THE STREET. NOW HE BEGGED TO SEE ME! BUT I KNEW IT WAS NO GOOD.

THAT SUMMER I LEFT FOR NEW YORK ON THE *LOVE HAPPY* TOUR.

.....Marilyn Monroe is a twenty-one year old from Van Nuys California with a tiny waist, a 36 inch braline and long pretty legs.... Earle Wilson

I POSED FOR HUNDREDS OF PHOTOS...

ALL PROMOTING ONE THING OR ANOTHER.

PHOTOPLAY'S "DREAM HOUSE"

Marilyn Monroe, the hottest thing in Hollywood, cooling off. Miss Monroe stars in the Marx Brother's film *Love Happy*.

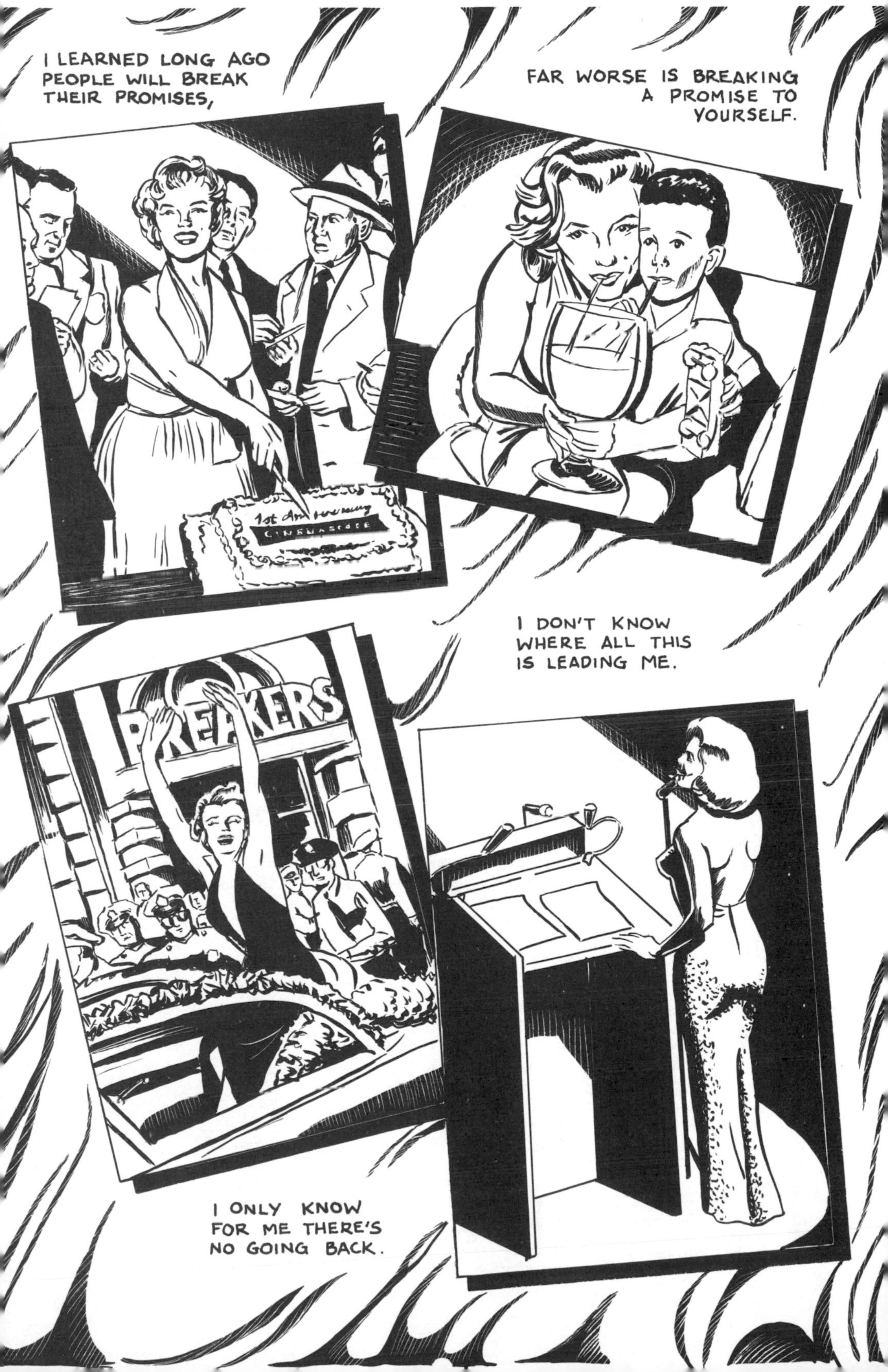
I LEARNED LONG AGO PEOPLE WILL BREAK THEIR PROMISES,
FAR WORSE IS BREAKING A PROMISE TO YOURSELF.
I DON'T KNOW WHERE ALL THIS IS LEADING ME.
BREAKERS
I ONLY KNOW FOR ME THERE'S NO GOING BACK.

EARLY IN 1949, I WAS MODELING AT THE RACQUET CLUB IN PALM SPRINGS TO TIDE ME OVER BETWEEN AUDITIONS. IT WAS THERE I STARTED ON THE PATH TO STARDOM WITH——

The Man Who Knew Me Too Well

HELLO, IT'S MISS MONROE, ISN'T IT?

YES, IT IS.

I'M AN ADMIRER OF YOURS.

I SAW YOUR BIT IN *LOVE HAPPY*. YOU LITERALLY WALKED AWAY WITH THE FILM.

I'M SURPRISED ANYONE SAW THAT MOVIE. THEY SAY IT WAS THE WORST MOVIE THE MARX BROTHERS MADE.

MY NAME IS JOHNNY HYDE. I'M WITH THE WILLIAM MORRIS AGENCY.

HAVE DINNER WITH ME TONIGHT, WE CAN DISCUSS YOUR FUTURE.

FROM THE BEGINNING JOHNNY WAS DIFFERENT. HE DIDN'T DO ALL THE TALKING. PRETTY SOON I FOUND MYSELF TELLING HIM ALL ABOUT MY LIFE, MY DISAPPOINTMENTS.

IT'S HARD FOR A STAR TO GET AN EATING JOB. A STAR IS ONLY GOOD AS A STAR. YOU DON'T FIT ANYTHING LESS.

I'M SERIOUS!

I'VE KNOWN EVERYONE IN THE BUSINESS, AND YOU'VE GOT STAR QUALITY. YOU COULD BE ANOTHER HARLOW.

YOU'D LIKE THAT, WOULDN'T YOU?

YES, MORE THAN ANYTHING.

NEXT DAY | WHEN WE GET BACK TO HOLLYWOOD I'M GOING TO MAKE IT MY BUSINESS THAT YOU ARE SEEN AT EVERY PREMIER, EVERY PARTY, EVERY CLUB...

YOU'RE GOING TO BE THE TALK OF THE TOWN.

JOHNNY WAS TRUE TO HIS WORD. IN A FEW MONTHS WE WERE BOTH THE TALK OF THE TOWN. AT ROMANOFF'S IN HOLLYWOOD—

LOOK AT THEM! HE JUST COMES UP TO HER BOSOM.

BUT WHAT A VIEW!

SHE'S THIRTY YEARS YOUNGER THAN HE IS!

HE'S MAKING A FOOL OF HIMSELF.

I FEEL SORRY FOR HIS WIFE.

BUT JOHNNY DIDN'T CARE WHAT PEOPLE SAID. HE HAD FAITH IN ME. IN A PRODUCER'S OFFICE—

YES, WE SCREENED HER FILM CLIPS.

I'M SORRY, WE FEEL MISS MONROE HAS NO STAR POTENTIAL.

POOR BASTARD. THAT HUSTLER REALLY HAS HIM BY THE BALLS.

I WAS HIS MISTRESS, ALL HOLLYWOOD KNEW ABOUT IT.

JOHNNY LEFT HIS WIFE AND TWO SONS. HE BOUGHT A HOUSE IN
BEVERLY HILLS AND I MOVED IN WITH HIM. IN THE DINING ROOM JOHNNY
INSTALLED FOUR WHITE LEATHER BOOTHS AND A DANCE FLOOR. IT WAS
OUR OWN PRIVATE ROMANOFF'S.

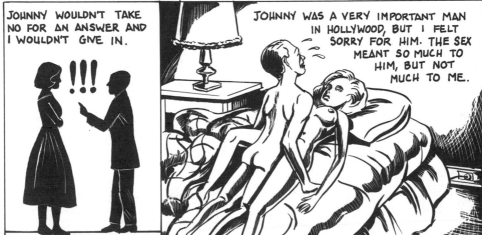

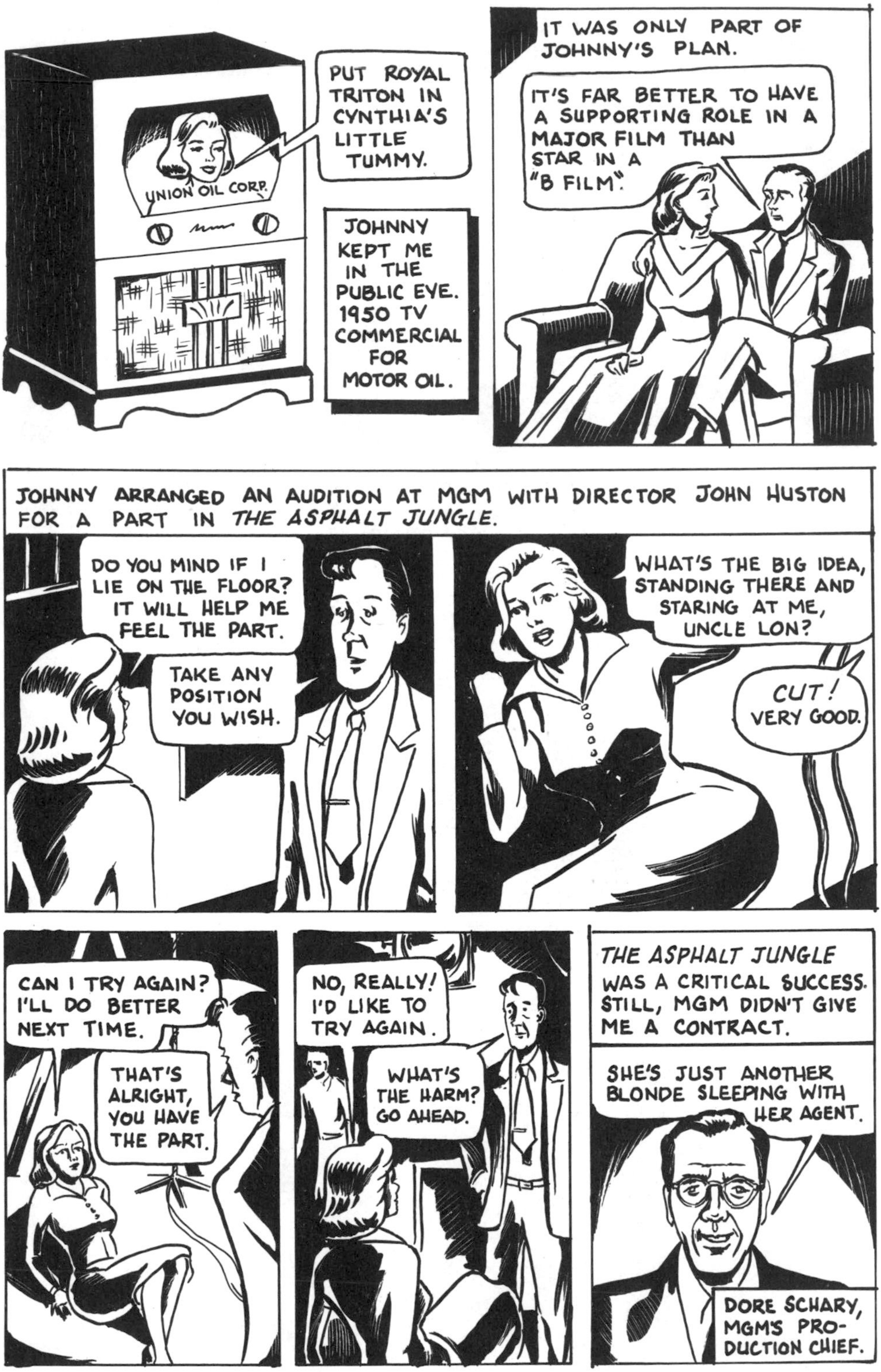
UNION OIL CORP.
PUT ROYAL TRITON IN CYNTHIA'S LITTLE TUMMY.
JOHNNY KEPT ME IN THE PUBLIC EYE. 1950 TV COMMERCIAL FOR MOTOR OIL.
IT WAS ONLY PART OF JOHNNY'S PLAN.
IT'S FAR BETTER TO HAVE A SUPPORTING ROLE IN A MAJOR FILM THAN STAR IN A "B FILM".
JOHNNY ARRANGED AN AUDITION AT MGM WITH DIRECTOR JOHN HUSTON FOR A PART IN *THE ASPHALT JUNGLE*.
DO YOU MIND IF I LIE ON THE FLOOR? IT WILL HELP ME FEEL THE PART.
TAKE ANY POSITION YOU WISH.
WHAT'S THE BIG IDEA, STANDING THERE AND STARING AT ME, UNCLE LON?
CUT! VERY GOOD.
CAN I TRY AGAIN? I'LL DO BETTER NEXT TIME.
THAT'S ALRIGHT, YOU HAVE THE PART.
NO, REALLY! I'D LIKE TO TRY AGAIN.
WHAT'S THE HARM? GO AHEAD.
THE ASPHALT JUNGLE WAS A CRITICAL SUCCESS. STILL, MGM DIDN'T GIVE ME A CONTRACT.
SHE'S JUST ANOTHER BLONDE SLEEPING WITH HER AGENT.
DORE SCHARY, MGM'S PRODUCTION CHIEF.

ABOUT THIS TIME JOHNNY HAD A HEART ATTACK.

MARILYN, I'M NOT GOING TO LIVE LONG. I WORRY ABOUT YOU.

WHAT'S GOING TO HAPPEN TO YOU AFTER I'M GONE?

PLEASE, JOHNNY.

I'M A RICH MAN. MARRY ME AND YOU'LL NEVER WORRY ABOUT MONEY AGAIN.

DON'T TALK LIKE THAT. REST JOHNNY, YOU'LL GET BETTER.

BUT I WAS REALLY FRIGHTENED.

WHEN HE RETURNED HOME, JOHNNY BEGGED ME DAY AND NIGHT TO MARRY HIM. THE THOUGHT OF SEX ALARMED ME.

I DECIDED IT WAS BEST THAT I MOVED.

I'LL COME BACK, SOON AS YOU RECOVER. I PROMISE.

DESPITE THE WARNINGS, JOHNNY WORKED HARDER THAN EVER TO PROMOTE ME. WITH ALAN HALE JR., *HOME TOWN STORY.*

THANKS TO JOHNNY I WAS NEVER WITHOUT WORK. WITH DICK POWELL IN *RIGHT CROSS.*

JOHNNY TOOK ME TO TWENTIETH CENTURY FOX. I GOT A PART IN *ALL ABOUT EVE.* I PLAY MISS CASWELL, A STUDENT OF "THE COPACABANA SCHOOL OF DRAMATIC ART." WITH ANNE BAXTER, BETTE DAVIS AND GEORGE SANDERS.

TWENTIETH CENTURY FOX WOULDN'T GIVE ME A CONTRACT, EITHER.

I SEE NOTHING REMARKABLE IN MISS MONROE.

DARRYL ZANUCK, STUDIO HEAD

JOHNNY PERSISTED, UNTIL ZANUCK GAVE ME A SCREEN TEST FOR A DRAMA, *COLD SHOULDER*

EVERY DAY I KEPT A PHYSICAL REGIMEN.

JOHNNY ARRANGED PLASTIC SURGERY TO IMPROVE MY PROFILE.

REMOVE → SMALL BUMP

ADD PROSTHESIS UNDER LIP →

I ALSO BEGAN TO STUDY ACTING WITH MICHAEL CHEKOV, THE NEPHEW OF THE FAMOUS PLAYWRIGHT, ANTON CHEKOV.

YOUR BODY IS AN INSTRUMENT FOR EXPRESSING CREATIVE IDEAS. YOU MUST STRIVE FOR HARMONY BETWEEN BODY AND PSYCHOLOGY.

ACTING IS GOOD, BUT NOT NECESSARY TO BECOMING A STAR.

JOHNNY.

IT'S MORE IMPORTANT THAT YOU KEEP YOUR FIGURE.

I TAKE CARE OF MYSELF! YOU'RE JUST JEALOUS OF THE TIME I'M AWAY FROM YOU!

DO YOU KNOW WHY I DO ALL THIS FOR YOU? TO GIVE YOU THE ONE THING YOU WANT MORE THAN ANYTHING ELSE, EVEN MORE THAN BEING AN ACTRESS.

YOU WANT TO BE A STAR. YOU NEED TO BE A STAR, OR ELSE YOU'LL NEVER BE HAPPY.

JOHNNY KNEW ME TOO WELL.

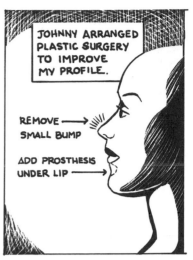

JOHNNY INVITED ME TO STAY WITH HIM WHILE MY PLASTIC SURGERY HEALED.

I LOOK LIKE CLAUDE RAINS IN *THE INVISIBLE MAN.*

I BEGAN TO NOTICE CHANGES IN JOHNNY. HE HAD LOST WEIGHT.

HE COULD NO LONGER CLIMB THE STAIRS.

DEAR, SWEET JOHNNY. ALTHOUGH I REFUSED TO MARRY HIM, HE NEVER STOPPED LOVING ME, NEVER STOPPED WORKING FOR ME.

IT WAS DECEMBER. I WAS CHRISTMAS SHOPPING WHEN HE HAD HIS FINAL HEART ATTACK.

IT WAS ALL OVER BY THE TIME I REACHED THE HOSPITAL.

HIS WIFE'S LAWYERS HAD ME REMOVED FROM HIS HOUSE. SHE DIDN'T WANT ME AT THE FUNERAL, SO I PRETENDED I WAS A SERVANT.

PERHAPS YOU SHOULD LEAVE NOW, MISS.

TWENTIETH CENTURY FOX KEPT ME ON FOR ANOTHER MOVIE, *AS YOUNG AS YOU FEEL*. ONE DAY I HAD SOME VISITORS ON THE SET, ELIA KAZAN AND HIS FRIEND FROM NEW YORK.

SHE CAN'T STOP CRYING, IT PUFFS UP HER EYES.

MAYBE I CAN CHEER HER UP. WHERE IS SHE?

PROBABLY OFF IN A CORNER SOMEWHERE.

MARILYN HONEY, WHAT'S THE MATTER?

OH ELIA, I MUST LOOK AWFUL.

HERE, DRY YOUR EYES.

WHO'S YOUR FRIEND?

THIS IS ARTHUR MILLER, HE'S A PLAYWRIGHT.

FORGIVE ME, MR. MILLER. A DEAR FRIEND OF MINE RECENTLY DIED.

I'M SORRY IF I INTRUDED.

THAT'S ALRIGHT, I'M ALWAYS HAPPY TO MEET A FRIEND OF ELIA'S.

I HOPE WE MEET AGAIN, WHEN I'M MORE MYSELF.

PROPERTY OF TCF

I CONTINUED WORKING AT FOX FROM WEEK TO WEEK. FINALLY, I GOT A SHORT TERM CONTRACT. THANKS TO JOHNNY, I HAD A FOOTHOLD.

WITH ALBERT DEKKER IN AS YOUNG AS YOU FEEL.

THE FILM ALL ABOUT EVE WAS A BIG HIT. EVERYONE SAID I FIT THE ROLE OF DIMWITTED MISS CASWELL TO A "T." THEY SHOULD HAVE CAST ME AS EVE.

I'VE LISTENED FROM BACKSTAGE TO PEOPLE APPLAUD. IT'S LIKE WAVES OF LOVE... HUNDREDS OF PEOPLE LOVE YOU, THEIR EYES SHINE, YOU'VE PLEASED THEM, THEY WANT YOU, YOU BELONG. JUST THAT ALONE IS WORTH ANYTHING.

ANNE BAXTER AS "EVE"

FIVE MONTHS INTO MY NEW CONTRACT AT FOX. I'M CAST IN TWO MOVIES SO BAD THEY NEED A BLONDE (ME) TO KEEP THE AUDIENCE AWAKE.

MY PARTS ARE NEVER IMPORTANT, BUT I'M ALWAYS ON THE POSTER. IT'S GETTING HARDER TO BELIEVE I'M PAYING MY DUES, THAT THIS IS LEADING SOMEWHERE,

STILL, I CONTINUE TO STUDY ACTING WITH MICHAEL CHEKHOV.

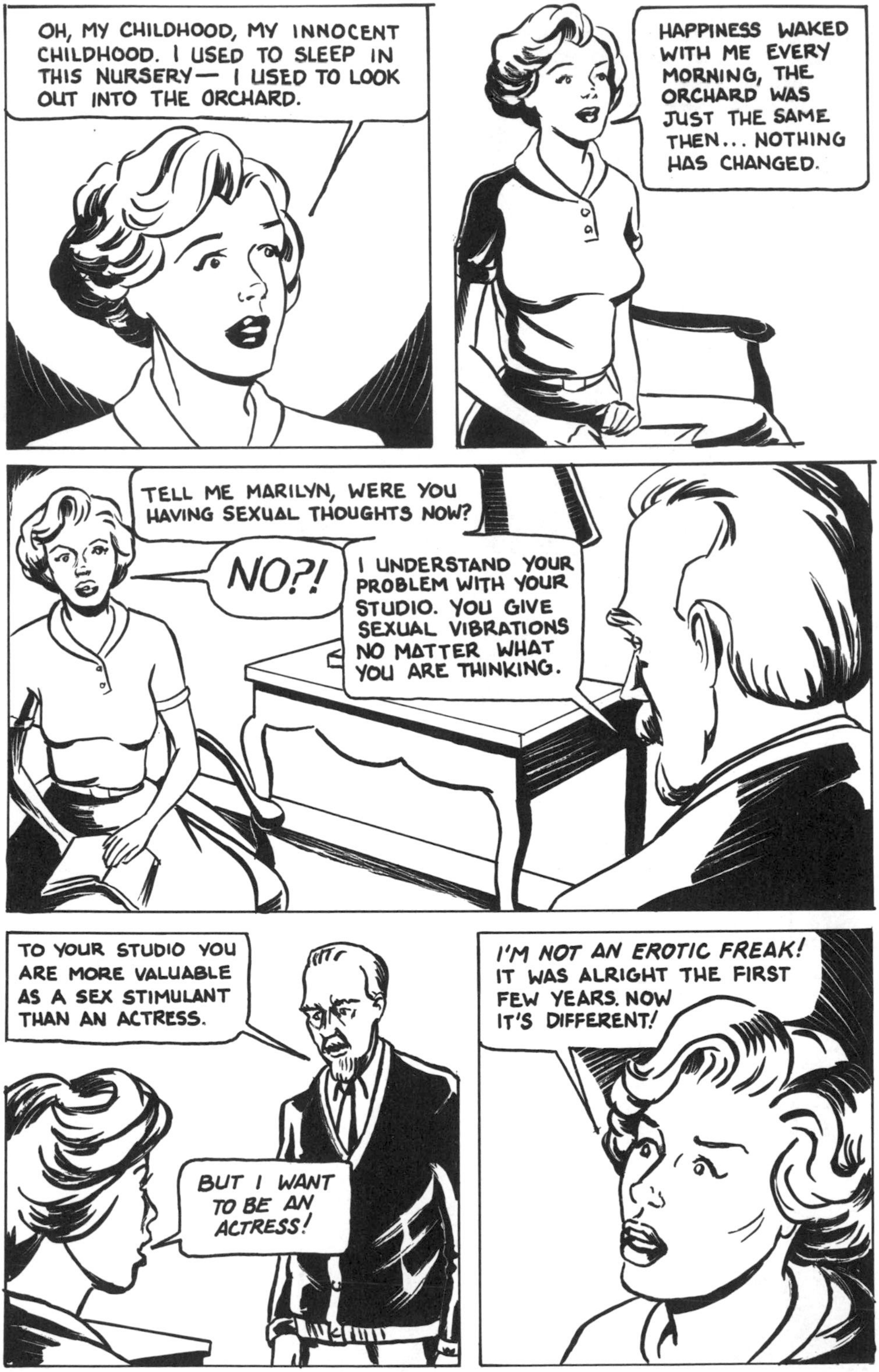
OH, MY CHILDHOOD, MY INNOCENT CHILDHOOD. I USED TO SLEEP IN THIS NURSERY— I USED TO LOOK OUT INTO THE ORCHARD.
HAPPINESS WAKED WITH ME EVERY MORNING, THE ORCHARD WAS JUST THE SAME THEN... NOTHING HAS CHANGED.
TELL ME MARILYN, WERE YOU HAVING SEXUAL THOUGHTS NOW?
NO?!
I UNDERSTAND YOUR PROBLEM WITH YOUR STUDIO. YOU GIVE SEXUAL VIBRATIONS NO MATTER WHAT YOU ARE THINKING.
TO YOUR STUDIO YOU ARE MORE VALUABLE AS A SEX STIMULANT THAN AN ACTRESS.
BUT I WANT TO BE AN ACTRESS!
I'M NOT AN EROTIC FREAK! IT WAS ALRIGHT THE FIRST FEW YEARS. NOW IT'S DIFFERENT!

FIVE YEARS EARLIER.

AT THE END OF SIX MONTHS MY CONTRACT WILL BE UP FOR RENEWAL. DARRYL ZANUCK IS PRODUCTION CHIEF AND THE SAME MAN WHO ONCE FIRED ME FOR BEING "UNPHOTOGENIC."

DARRYL ZANUCK

I NEED TO SEE MR. ZANUCK.

DO YOU HAVE AN APPOINTMENT?

NO, BUT IT'S VERY IMPORTANT.

YOU SEE, I WAS A CONTRACT PLAYER HERE AND I WANT TO KNOW WHY MR. ZANUCK FIRED ME.

I'M SORRY, BUT MR. ZANUCK IS IN SUN VALLEY.

I DIDN'T GIVE UP. I CAME BACK A WEEK LATER.

 I'M SORRY, MR. ZANUCK IS STILL IN SUN VALLEY.

 YOU MEAN HE'S ALWAYS IN SUN VALLEY WHERE A CONTRACT PLAYER IS CONCERNED.

 PERHAPS IF YOU CALLED FIRST...

NATURALLY, I'M WORRIED NOW THAT MY CONTRACT IS UP AGAIN.

 DON'T WORRY! HISTORY ISN'T GOING TO REPEAT ITSELF.

 YOU'VE FOUND YOUR NICHE. I'M JUST A CELLULOID APHRODISIAC!

I'M GETTING FAN MAIL, THOUSANDS OF LETTERS. I COULD BE A STAR, IF GIVEN HALF A CHANCE!

 WHAT'S WRONG WITH ME? WHY DOESN'T HE LIKE ME? LOOK AT IT THIS WAY.

 ZANUCK IS A SMALL TOWN BOY FROM NEBRASKA. HE LIKES EXOTIC, FOREIGN WOMEN, NOT ALL-AMERICAN GIRLS LIKE YOU.

 YOU'RE JUST NOT HIS TYPE! THERE HAS TO BE SOMETHING I CAN DO.

EVERY YEAR THE STUDIO INVITES EXHIBITORS FROM ALL OVER THE COUNTRY TO HOLLYWOOD.

A BIG PARTY IS HELD IN THEIR HONOR. ALL THE EX- CUTIVES AND STARS DO THEIR BEST TO IMPRESS THEM.

SPYROS SKOURAS, DARYL ZANUCK'S BOSS, FLEW IN FROM NEW YORK. THIS PARTY IS THAT IMPORTANT.

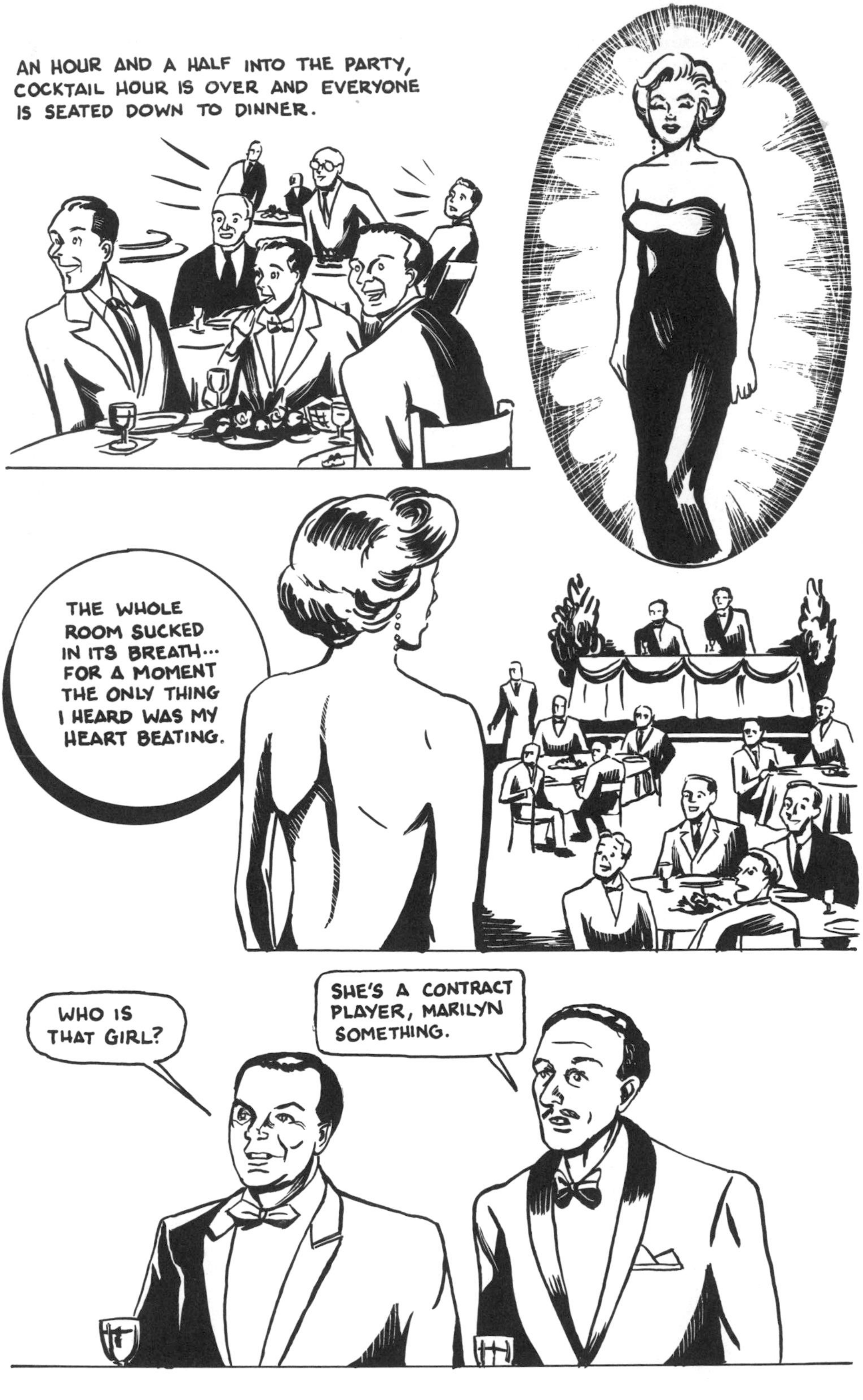

AN HOUR AND A HALF INTO THE PARTY, COCKTAIL HOUR IS OVER AND EVERYONE IS SEATED DOWN TO DINNER.
THE WHOLE ROOM SUCKED IN ITS BREATH... FOR A MOMENT THE ONLY THING I HEARD WAS MY HEART BEATING.
WHO IS THAT GIRL?
SHE'S A CONTRACT PLAYER, MARILYN SOMETHING.

WHAT FILMS IS SHE SCHEDULED TO APPEAR IN?

SHE'S NOT CURRENTLY SCHEDULED.

THE EXHIBITORS LIKE HER.

IF THE EXHIBITORS LIKE HER, THE PUBLIC LIKES HER.

MR. SKOUROS PERSONALLY ESCORTED ME TO HIS TABLE.

AND SEATED ME BESIDE HIM.

THAT NIGHT
I LEFT WITH
MR. SKOURAS.
NEXT MORNING
HE ORDERED
THE STUDIO
TO FEATURE
ME IN AS
MANY FILMS
AS POSSIBLE

MY CONTRACT IS SECURED
FOR ANOTHER SEVEN YEARS.

NIAGARA
1953

THE LAST ROADBLOCK
TO STARDOM, IF NOT
ACTING, HAD BEEN
REMOVED.

THERE'S NO BUSINESS
LIKE SHOW BUSINESS
1954

MY LIFE WOULD
BE CHANGED
FOREVER.

THREE YEARS LATER: IN 1954 AMERICANS WERE BUYING SPLIT LEVEL HOUSES, CARS WITH TAIL FINS AND TELEVISION SETS. DESPERATE TO HOLD AUDIENCES, HOLLYWOOD'S GREATEST DRAW WAS THE SAME WOMAN IT HAD ONCE REJECTED.

④

MARILYN MONROE IS REPORTED TO HAVE SAID, "AFTER ALL I'VE COME

UP FROM WAY DOWN

A PARTY WAS HELD IN MY HONOR CELEBRATING THE COMPLETION OF *THE SEVEN YEAR ITCH*.

THE ELITE OF HOLLYWOOD WERE THERE, HUMPHREY BOGART...

LAUREN BACALL AND SWIFTY LAZAR...

GARY COOPER, SUSAN HAYWARD, CLIFTON WEBB...

AND BEST OF ALL, CLARK GABLE.

EVEN THE STUDIO BOSSES CAME,

JACK WARNER of WARNER BROTHERS

SAMUEL GOLDWYN of MGM

AND MY BOSS, DARRYL ZANUCK

SHE CAN'T REMEMBER HER LINES, SHE ARRIVES AT THE SET LATE...

SHE'S SENSATIONAL! SHE'S WORTH THE TROUBLE!

MARILYN!

I'VE SEEN THE FIRST COMPLETED REELS. YOU LOOK MAGNIFICENT.

THANK-YOU, MR. ZANUCK.

IT'S BECAUSE OF BILLY WILDER, HE'S SUCH A WONDERFUL DIRECTOR.

I WANT TO WORK WITH BILLY AGAIN, BUT HE'S DOING THE CHARLES LINDBERGH STORY NEXT AND HE WON'T LET ME PLAY LINDBERGH!

LATER I DANCED WITH SIDNEY SKOLSKY.

I NEVER THOUGHT THEY'D ALL COME, HONEST. I FEEL LIKE CINDERELLA.

CONGRATULATIONS! HONEY, YOU'VE ARRIVED.

MAY I CUT IN?

IT WAS CLARK GABLE.

I'VE ADMIRED YOU SINCE I WAS SEVEN. I WOULD LOVE TO DO A MOVIE WITH YOU.

I SAW GENTLEMEN PREFER BLONDES. I'D LIKE TO DO A MOVIE WITH YOU. YOU HAVE THE MAGIC.

BUT TO MY STUDIO I WAS ANYTHING BUT MAGIC.

A STRIPPER! YOU WANT ME TO PLAY A STRIPPER?!*

*HOW TO BE VERY, VERY POPULAR, FILMED IN 1955, STARING SHEREE NORTH.

YOU'RE MAKING ME INTO A CLICHE'! THE PUBLIC WILL TIRE OF ME IF I PLAY THE SAME ROLE OVER AND OVER.

WE'RE CASTING YOU IN A QUALITY PRODUCTION WE'RE INVESTING MILLIONS IN THIS FILM.

YOU PAY ME LIKE A SUPPORTING PLAYER.

WE ARE ONLY FULFILLING THE SALARY STATED IN YOUR CONTRACT.

THAT CONTRACT WAS MADE WHEN I WAS STARTING OUT IN THE BUSINESS.

I'M A STAR NOW! I MAKE A LOT OF MONEY FOR YOU!

THIS IS USELESS, MISS MONROE.

WE HAVE A BINDING CONTRACT.

YOU'RE TREATING ME LIKE A MONEY MACHINE.

IT'S NOT FAIR!

NEVERTHELESS, WE EXPECT YOU TO REPORT TO THE SET ON TIME.

I CAN'T LET THEM GET AWAY WITH THIS.

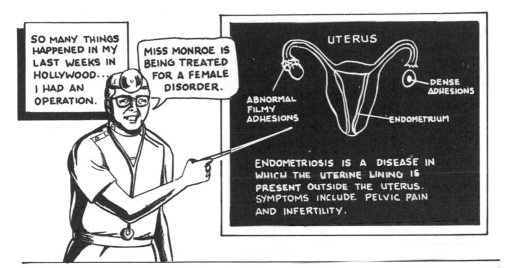

SO MANY THINGS HAPPENED IN MY LAST WEEKS IN HOLLYWOOD... I HAD AN OPERATION.

MISS MONROE IS BEING TREATED FOR A FEMALE DISORDER.

UTERUS

DENSE ADHESIONS

ABNORMAL FILMY ADHESIONS

ENDOMETRIUM

ENDOMETRIOSIS IS A DISEASE IN WHICH THE UTERINE LINING IS PRESENT OUTSIDE THE UTERUS. SYMPTOMS INCLUDE PELVIC PAIN AND INFERTILITY.

MY EX-HUSBAND, JOE DIMAGGIO, DROVE ME TO THE HOSPITAL.

THE WHOLE TIME HE WAS NEVER FAR AWAY.

SOMEHOW THE PRESS LEARNED OF THIS.

THEY WERE LAYING IN WAIT WHEN I WAS RELEASED.

MARILYN, ARE YOU AND JOE GETTING BACK TOGETHER?

WE HAD BEEN DIVORCED FOR A MONTH, BUT JOE WAS STILL A PART OF MY LIFE.

MY FAVORITE SINGER CAME TO TOWN.

ELLA FITZGERALD! WE HAVE TO SEE HER. WHERE IS SHE SINGING?

ON THE WRONG SIDE OF THE TRACKS, I'M AFRAID.

ALL THE HOLLYWOOD CLUBS TURNED HER DOWN. YOU KNOW HOW IT IS.

THEY DON'T WANT NEGRO PERFORMERS.

WELL, I'M GOING TO DO SOMETHING ABOUT THAT.

I INVITED THE OWNER OF THE MOCAMBO TO SIT WITH US. WE STRUCK A DEAL.

IF YOU AGREE TO ENGAGE MISS FITZGERALD, I WILL ATTEND EVERY NIGHT.

THE PRESS WILL GO WILD. THE PUBLICITY WILL BE PRICELESS.

I'M SURE YOU'RE RIGHT!

BUT LET ME ASK YOU A QUESTION. WHY ARE YOU DOING THIS?

MISS FITZGERALD IS A FINE ARTIST. I ADMIRE HER VERY MUCH...

AND I KNOW WHAT IT IS TO BE AN UNDERDOG IN THIS TOWN.

HE HELD UP HIS END OF THE DEAL, I HELD UP MINE.

MISS FITZGERALD'S PERFORMANCES SOLD OUT EVERY NIGHT. SOON, OTHER NEGRO ENTERTAINERS FOLLOWED.

IF ONLY I COULD SOLVE MY OWN PROBLEMS SO EASILY.

MY LAST DAYS IN HOLLYWOOD WERE SO BUSY.

I POSED FOR PUBLICITY PICTURES FOR *THE SEVEN YEAR ITCH.*

I MET THE ENGLISH POET, EDITH SITWELL...

... AND I CONSPIRED WITH PHOTOGRAPHER MILTON GREENE TO LEAVE HOLLYWOOD AND SET UP MY OWN PRODUCTION COMPANY.

I GAVE UP THE LEASE OF MY HOUSE AND MOVED IN WITH MY OLD FRIEND AND FRED'S SISTER, MARY KARGER.

I HAD GONE UNDERGROUND.

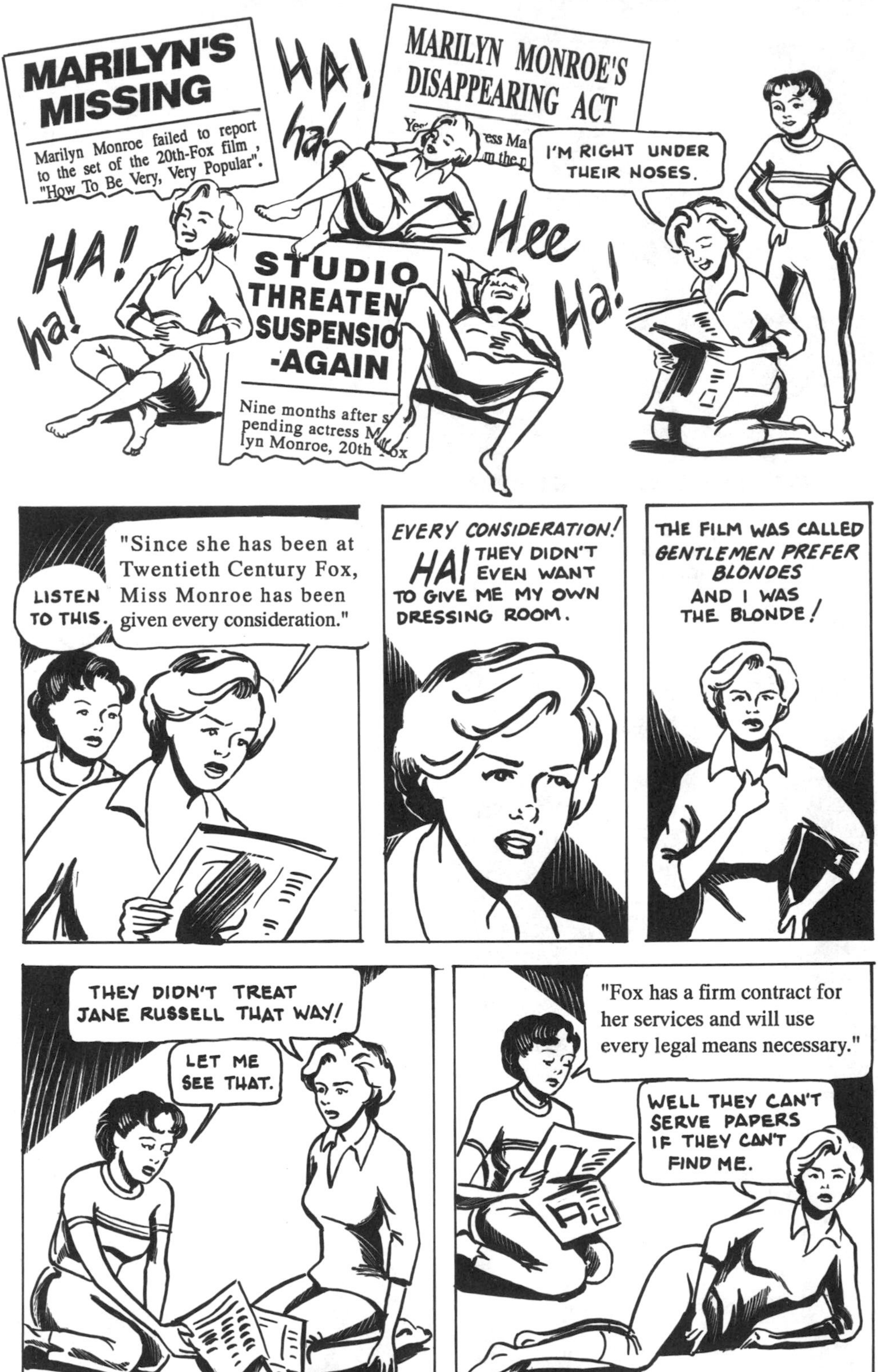
MARILYN'S MISSING
Marilyn Monroe failed to report to the set of the 20th-Fox film , "How To Be Very, Very Popular".
HA! ha!
MARILYN MONROE'S DISAPPEARING ACT
HA! ha!
STUDIO THREATEN SUSPENSIO -AGAIN
Nine months after s pending actress M lyn Monroe, 20th Fox
Hee Ha!
I'M RIGHT UNDER THEIR NOSES.
LISTEN TO THIS.
"Since she has been at Twentieth Century Fox, Miss Monroe has been given every consideration."
EVERY CONSIDERATION!
HA! THEY DIDN'T EVEN WANT TO GIVE ME MY OWN DRESSING ROOM.
THE FILM WAS CALLED GENTLEMEN PREFER BLONDES AND I WAS THE BLONDE!
THEY DIDN'T TREAT JANE RUSSELL THAT WAY!
LET ME SEE THAT.
"Fox has a firm contract for her services and will use every legal means necessary."
WELL THEY CAN'T SERVE PAPERS IF THEY CAN'T FIND ME.

AREN'T YOU EVEN A LITTLE BIT WORRIED?

MILTON GREENE AND I ARE SETTING UP OUR OWN PRODUCTION COMPANY.

THE PAPER WORK IS DONE AND OUR LAWYERS SAY FOX HAS BROKEN IT'S OWN CONTRACT.

BUT HONEY...

MILTON IS A PHOTOGRAPHER! WHAT DOES HE KNOW ABOUT SETTING UP A PRODUCTION COMPANY?

I HAVE FAITH IN MILTON AND MILTON HAS FAITH IN ME!

MARILYN — IT'S JUST THAT YOU'VE COME SO FAR... THERE'S NO LIMIT TO HOW FAR YOU CAN GO.

IF YOU LEAVE HOLLYWOOD NOW IT COULD BE THE END OF YOUR CAREER.

I KNOW.

BUT IF I STAY I'LL BECOME WHAT THEY THINK I AM, A DUMB BLONDE. I'M AN ACTRESS, I'M A PERSON. I HAVE TO GROW.

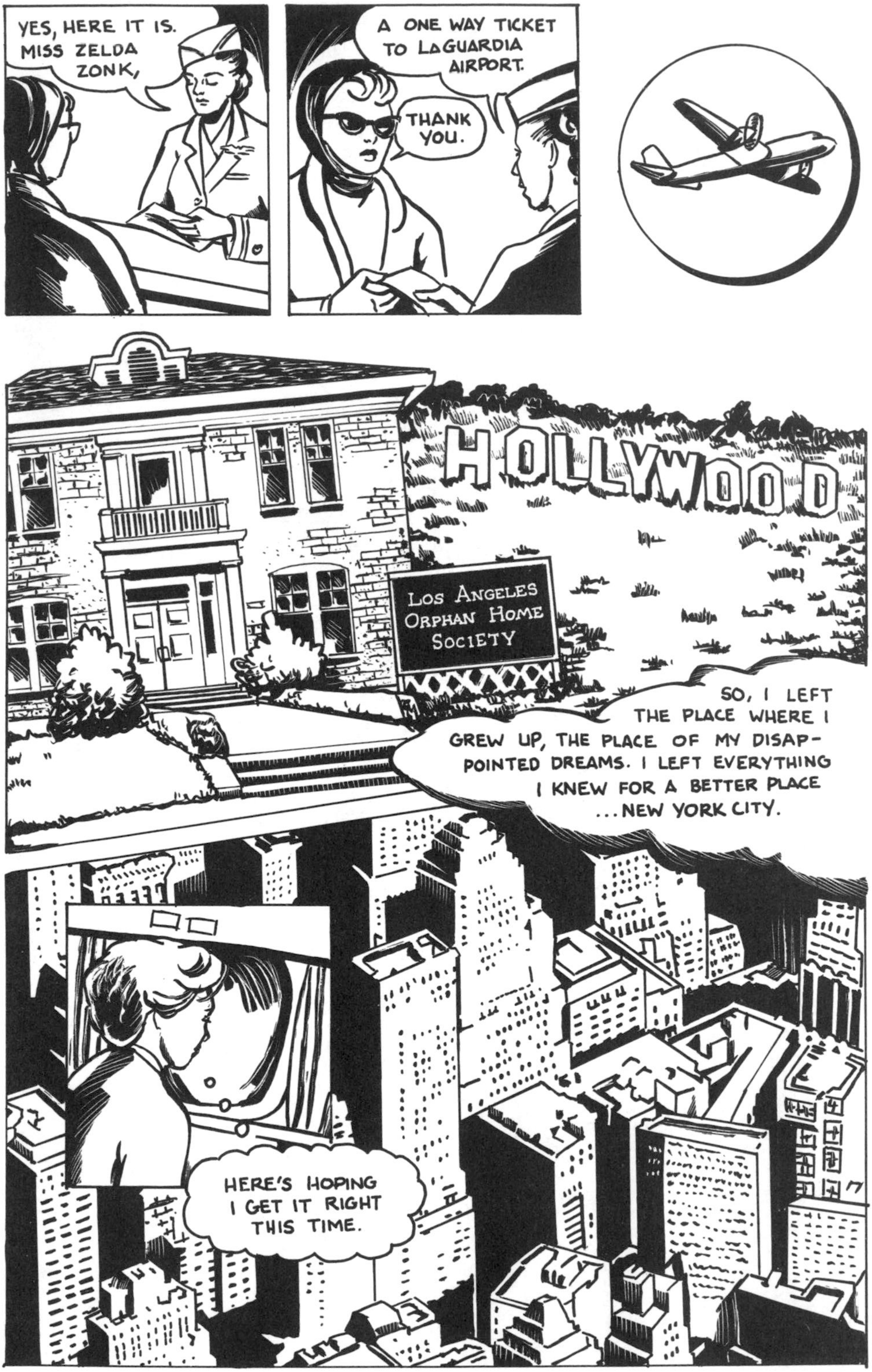
YES, HERE IT IS. MISS ZELDA ZONK,
A ONE WAY TICKET TO LaGUARDIA AIRPORT.
THANK YOU.
HOLLYWOOD
LOS ANGELES ORPHAN HOME SOCIETY
SO, I LEFT THE PLACE WHERE I GREW UP, THE PLACE OF MY DISAPPOINTED DREAMS. I LEFT EVERYTHING I KNEW FOR A BETTER PLACE ...NEW YORK CITY.
HERE'S HOPING I GET IT RIGHT THIS TIME.

I WAS MET BY MY NEW PARTNER, MILTON GREENE AND HIS WIFE, AMY.

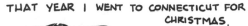

THAT YEAR I WENT TO CONNECTICUT FOR CHRISTMAS.

LOOK!

IT'S SNOWING!

HIDING COULD BE FUN.

YES, I UNDERSTAND, MR. HOPE. YOU WISH TO FIND MISS MONROE.

IS THAT BOB HOPE!

TELL ME, WHY ARE YOU CALLING? HAS MISS MONROE BEEN LOST?

OK GIRLS, HAVE YOUR FUN. JUST AS LONG AS WE KEEP THE ELEMENT OF SURPRISE.

Ha ha HA! HEE he ha

THE HOUNDS HAVE PICKED UP THE SCENT. WE CAN'T KEEP MARILYN A SECRET MUCH LONGER.

RING

DON'T WORRY. WE WON'T SLIP UP.

RING

NO, I'M VERY SORRY.

WHEN THE TIME COMES TO ANNOUNCE MARILYN MONROE PRODUCTIONS, YOU'LL MAKE YOUR ENTRANCE IN STYLE.

WE NEED INVESTORS AND YOUR FAME IS OUR GREATEST ASSET. YOU'RE GOING TO LIVE AND LOOK LIKE A MOVIE STAR.

WE DON'T KNOW HOW SHE CAN BE REACHED... I'M SORRY.

YOU'LL NEED TO STAY VISIBLE.

SHREE

THAT WAS FRANK SINATRA!

HE SAYS JOE DIMAGGIO IS FRANTIC TO FIND YOU.

OH, JOE.

I'M SORRY I HAD TO DO THIS TO JOE. WELL, IT COULDN'T BE HELPED.

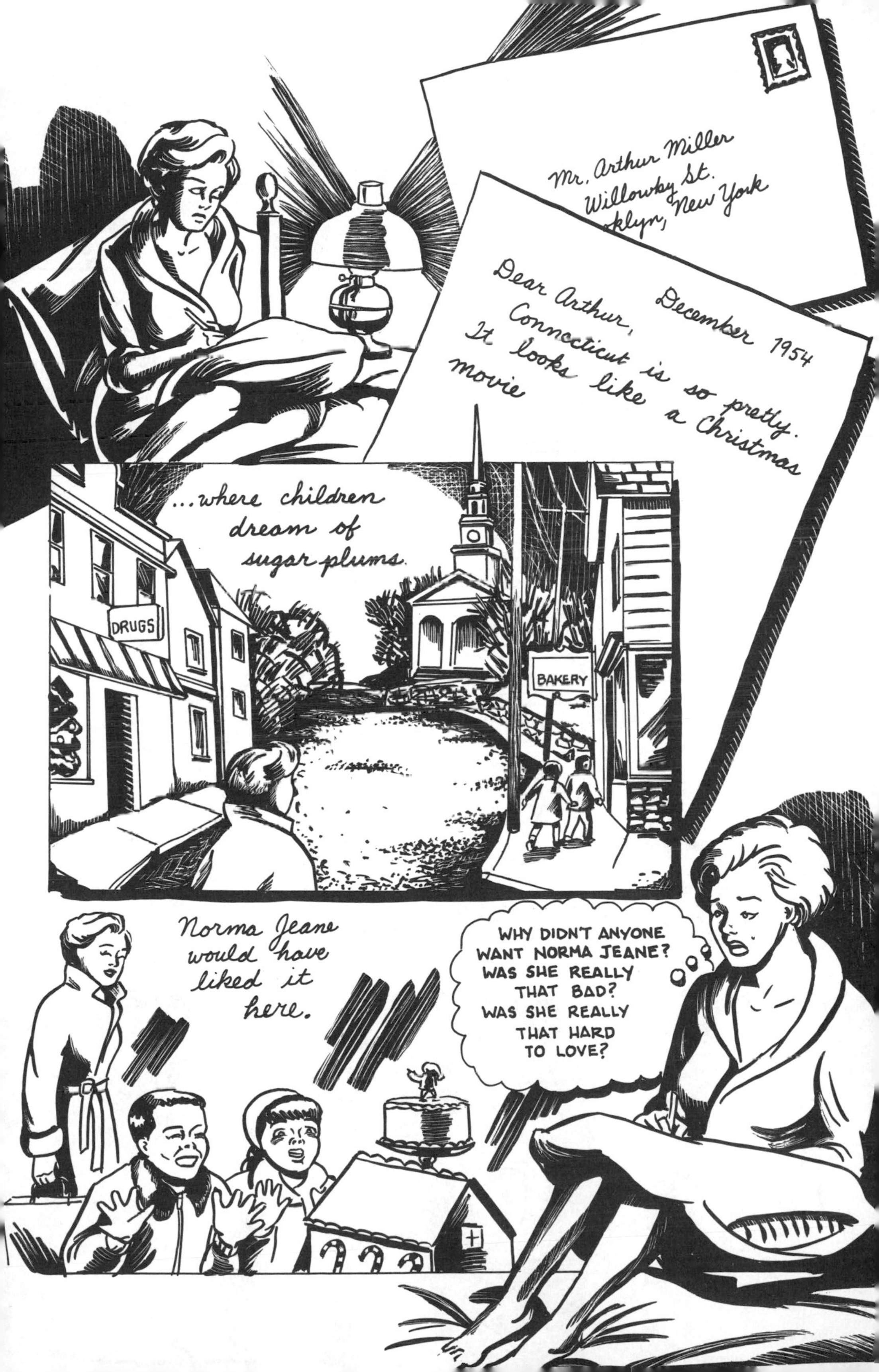
Mr. Arthur Miller
Willowky St.
klyn, New York
Dear Arthur, December 1954
Connecticut is so pretty.
It looks like a Christmas
movie
...where children
dream of
sugar plums.
DRUGS
BAKERY
Norma Jeane
would have
liked it
here.
WHY DIDN'T ANYONE
WANT NORMA JEANE?
WAS SHE REALLY
THAT BAD?
WAS SHE REALLY
THAT HARD
TO LOVE?

Everyone wants Marilyn, though. Connecticut is the last place anyone would expect to find me.

Imagine Lorelei Lee at the hardware store,

Pola at the A & P.

At night I read in my room. I've read about Josephine Bonaparte. Now I am reading about Isadora Duncan

...rdw...
...t the A&T
...night I read in ...
...om. I've read about
Josephine Bonaparte. Now
I'm reading about
Isador... ...can.
These women inspire me because they turned their lives around, as I hope to do.
I am trying to build a good opinion of myself. Your kindness means everything to me.
I hope we will meet again soon. I kept all your letters. I often think of you.
SHOULD I SAY THAT? HE'S A DECENT MAN. HE'S STILL MARRIED.
PERHAPS I'M BEING TOO PUSHY.
Rx
Rx
BUT WHEN WILL I SEE HIM AGAIN?
I HAVE TO SEE HIM AGAIN. I JUST HAVE TO.

IN JANUARY WE INVITED EIGHTY REPORTERS, PHOTOGRAPHERS, AND POTENTIAL INVESTORS TO A NEWS CONFERENCE.

I AM PLEASED TO ANNOUNCE THE FORMATION OF *MARILYN MONROE PRODUCTIONS*. I AM THE PRESIDENT, AND THIS IS MY PARTNER AND VICE PRESIDENT, MILTON GREENE.

MARILYN MONROE PRODUCTIONS WILL GO INTO ALL FIELDS OF ENTERTAINMENT. WE PLAN ON FC... OF TALENT...

MISS MONROE!

HOW WILL THIS EFFECT YOUR CONTRACT WITH TWENTIETH CENTURY FOX?

AS MISS MONROE'S COUNSEL-OR, I'D LIKE TO ANSWER THAT.

HER CONTRACT WITH TWENTIETH CENTURY FOX IS INVALID. FOX VIOLATED ITS OWN TERMS BY...

MARILYN! IT'S BEEN REPORTED YOU WISH TO PLAY *THE BROTHERS KARAMOZOV.*

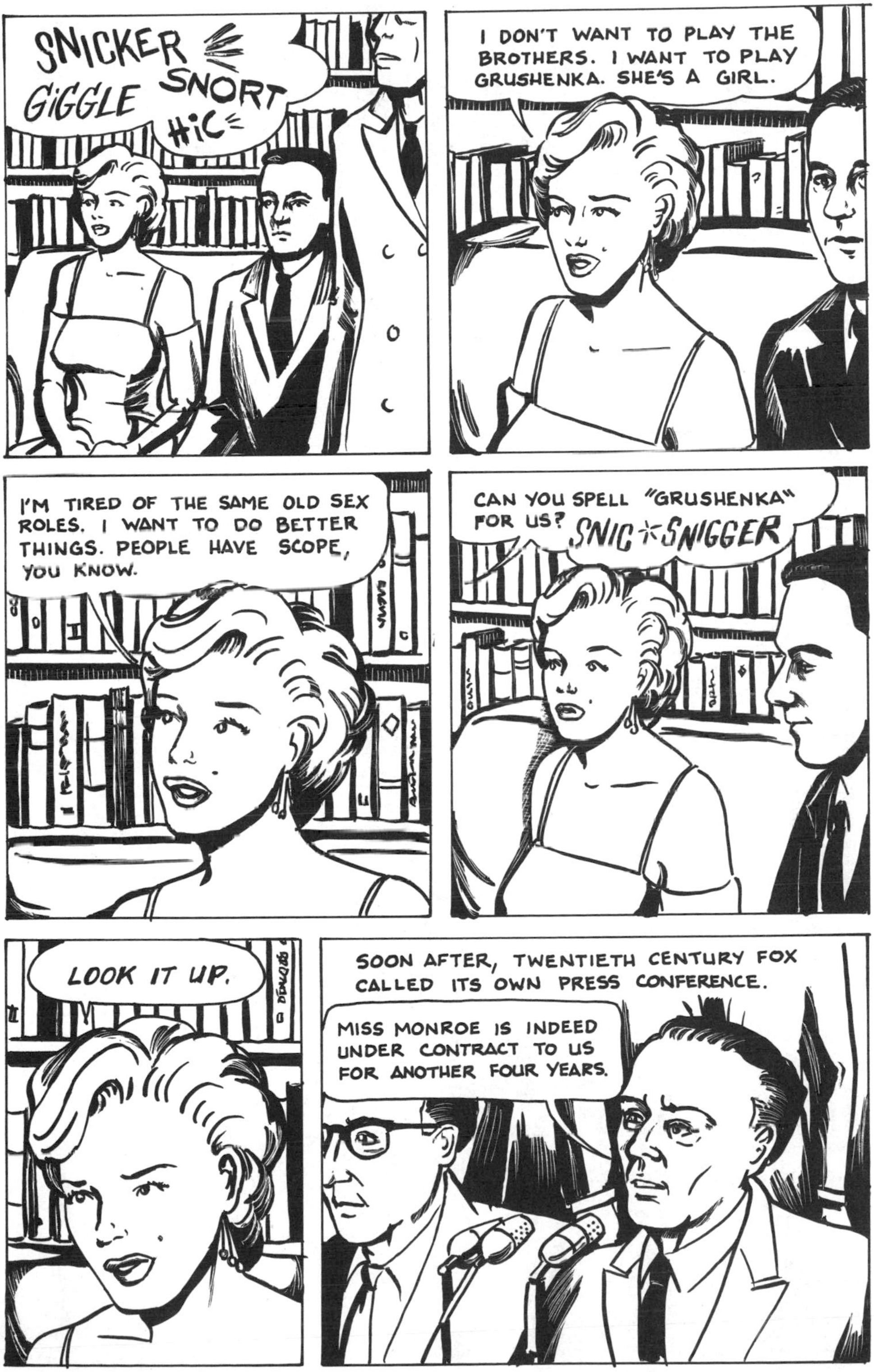
SNICKER GIGGLE SNORT HiC
I DON'T WANT TO PLAY THE BROTHERS. I WANT TO PLAY GRUSHENKA. SHE'S A GIRL.
I'M TIRED OF THE SAME OLD SEX ROLES. I WANT TO DO BETTER THINGS. PEOPLE HAVE SCOPE, YOU KNOW.
CAN YOU SPELL "GRUSHENKA" FOR US?
SNIC SNIGGER
LOOK IT UP.
SOON AFTER, TWENTIETH CENTURY FOX CALLED ITS OWN PRESS CONFERENCE.
MISS MONROE IS INDEED UNDER CONTRACT TO US FOR ANOTHER FOUR YEARS.

WHILE THE LAWYERS BATTLED OVER MY CONTRACT I HAD NO PROFESSIONAL OBLIGATIONS. I WAS FREE TO EXPLORE BROOKLYN WITH MY FRIEND, PHOTOGRAPHER SAM SHAW.

RING RING

HEY NORM! IT'S ME, SAM!

I'M WITH A MODEL AND WE'RE BOTH DRENCHED.

CAN WE COME OVER AND DRY OFF?

SURE, COME OVER.

WELCOME.

NORMAN, HEDDA, MEET "MARION".

YOU POOR THINGS, COME IN, I'LL GET YOU SOME SLIPPERS.

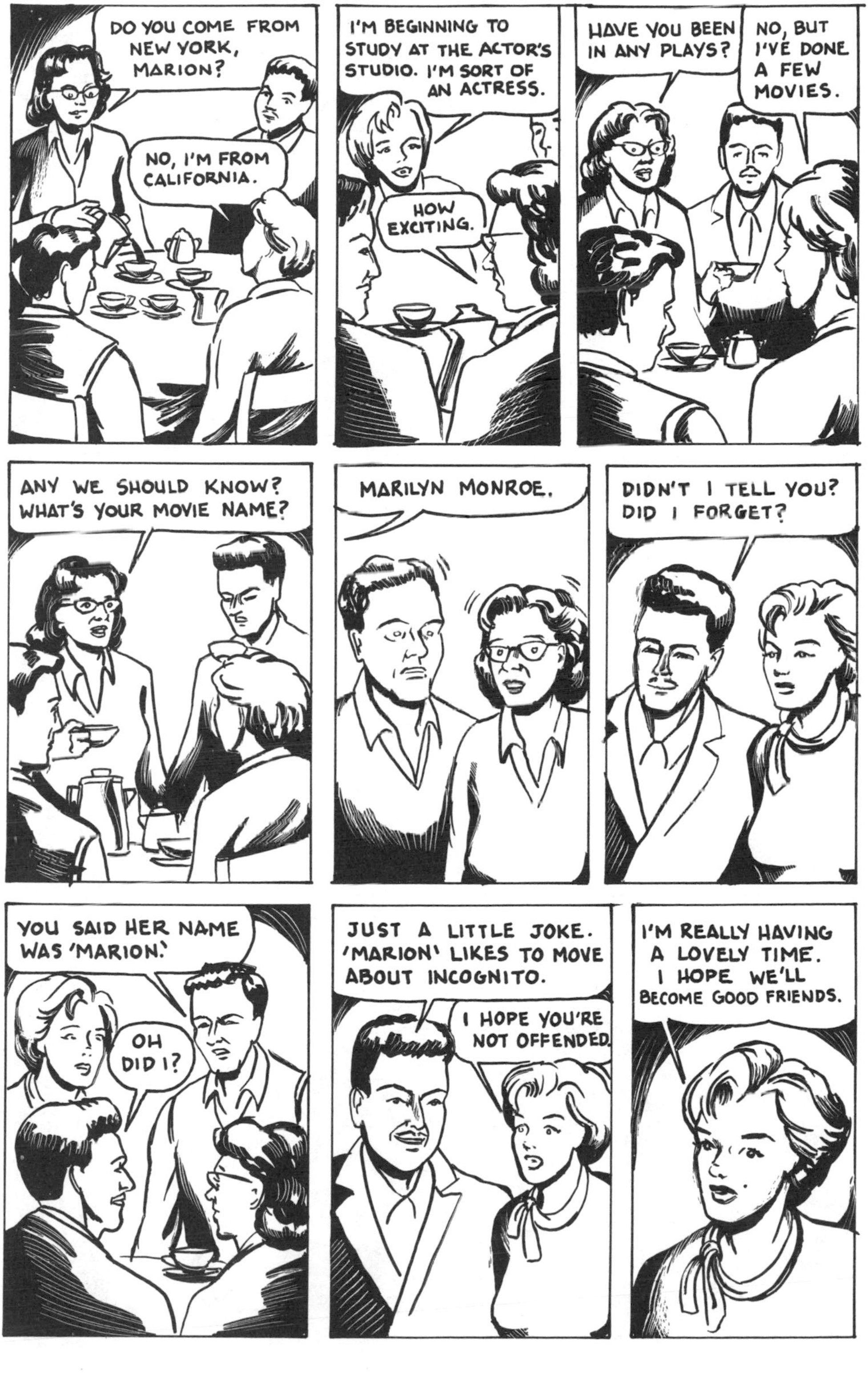
DO YOU COME FROM NEW YORK, MARION?
NO, I'M FROM CALIFORNIA.
I'M BEGINNING TO STUDY AT THE ACTOR'S STUDIO. I'M SORT OF AN ACTRESS.
HOW EXCITING.
HAVE YOU BEEN IN ANY PLAYS?
NO, BUT I'VE DONE A FEW MOVIES.
ANY WE SHOULD KNOW? WHAT'S YOUR MOVIE NAME?
MARILYN MONROE.
DIDN'T I TELL YOU? DID I FORGET?
YOU SAID HER NAME WAS 'MARION.'
OH DID I?
JUST A LITTLE JOKE. 'MARION' LIKES TO MOVE ABOUT INCOGNITO.
I HOPE YOU'RE NOT OFFENDED.
I'M REALLY HAVING A LOVELY TIME. I HOPE WE'LL BECOME GOOD FRIENDS.

THE GREAT ACTING INSTRUCTOR, LEE STRASBERG, CONSENTED TO GIVE ME PRIVATE LESSONS IN HIS HOME. I WAS VERY HONORED.

WHAT MOST IMPRESSED ME WHEN I MET YOU WAS YOUR SENSITIVITY. MOST ACTORS FROM HOLLYWOOD BECOME CALLOUSED AND UNREFLECTIVE.

IF ANYTHING YOUR EXPERIENCES HAVE MADE YOU MORE SENSITIVE.

IT'S REMARKABLE!

MOST PEOPLE DON'T THINK SO.

MOST PEOPLE THINK THERE'S SOMETHING WRONG WITH ME.

ONLY THE MOST JADED BELIEVE THAT.

YOUR SENSES ARE ALIVE, YOUR IMAGINATION IS ALIVE. AN ACTOR HAS NO GREATER ASSET.

I THINK YOU'RE READY TO START CLASSES AT THE STUDIO.

OH NO!

DON'T BE AFRAID TO MAKE MISTAKES! THE MEMBERS WILL HELP YOU, YOU'LL SEE.

BUT IN THE BEGINNING I SAT AT THE BACK OF THE ROOM, OBSERVING EVERYTHING AND SELDOM SPEAKING.

I WAS GRATEFUL FOR THE FRIENDSHIP OF NORMAN AND HEDDA ROSTEN. WITH THEM I COULD BE MYSELF.

I'M GLAD YOU MADE IT TONIGHT. THERE'S SOMEONE I WANT YOU TO MEET.

ARTHUR!

YOU KNOW EACH OTHER?!

I MET MARILYN IN HOLLYWOOD YEARS AGO.

APPARENTLY ARTHUR MADE A LASTING IMPRESSION.

WELL HE'S SO DIFFERENT FROM THOSE HOLLYWOOD TYPES.

AND I WAS GOING TO INTRODUCE YOU TO MY OLD COLLEGE FRIEND, THE FAMOUS PLAYWRIGHT.

?

IMAGINE! HERE WE ALL ARE, IN BROOKLYN. IT FEELS ALMOST LIKE FATE!

THANK-YOU FOR THE LETTER. I WAS FLATTERED YOU REMEMBERED ME.

NORMAN WAS RIGHT, YOU KNOW.

YOU DID MAKE A LASTING IMPRESSION.

I'D LIKE TO SEE YOU AGAIN. MAYBE JUST FOR A WALK.

I'D LIKE THAT.

AFTER DINNER WE TOOK TURNS READING POETRY.

NOW DON'T LOOK, JUST PICK A POEM AT RANDOM.

IT'S YEATS!

Never Give All the Heart
W.B. Yeats

FOR EVERYTHING THAT'S LOVELY IS

BUT A BRIEF DREAMY DELIGHT,

OH NEVER GIVE THE HEART OUTRIGHT.

AT THE ACTOR'S STUDIO

ALRIGHT CLASS, TELL ME WHAT YOU THINK OF THE SCENE WE JUST SAW.

I FOUND THE CHARACTER AND SITUATION VERY UNCLEAR.

I'D LIKE TO SEE THE SCENE IN SHARPER FOCUS.

YES, MARILYN.

I THINK THAT WAS THE POINT OF THE SCENE. THE CHARACTER WAS IN CONFUSION.

SOMETIMES LIFE ISN'T VERY CLEAR...

EXACTLY!

THAT'S EXACTLY THE MEANING OF THIS SCENE.

GOOD CALL.

THAT JUNE THE SEVEN YEAR ITCH WAS SCHEDULED FOR ITS BIG PREMIER. A FOUR STORY FIGURE OF MYSELF WAS ERECTED OVER TIMES SQUARE.

THE REACTION OF THE "MAN ON THE STREET."

I THINK IT'S VERY NICE, SOME GIRL.

I THINK IT'S VERY NICE, BUT I'D RATHER IT WERE ME.

WHAT DOES MARILYN MONROE HAVE THAT A MILLION OTHER WOMEN DON'T HAVE?

I THINK IT'S WONDERFUL. WONDERFUL, WONDERFUL, WONDERFUL.

IT'S PRETTY VULGAR, IF YOU ASK ME.

THAT'S HOW THEY THINK OF ME IN HOLLYWOOD, WITH MY SKIRT OVER MY HEAD.

ACTOR, ELI WALLACH

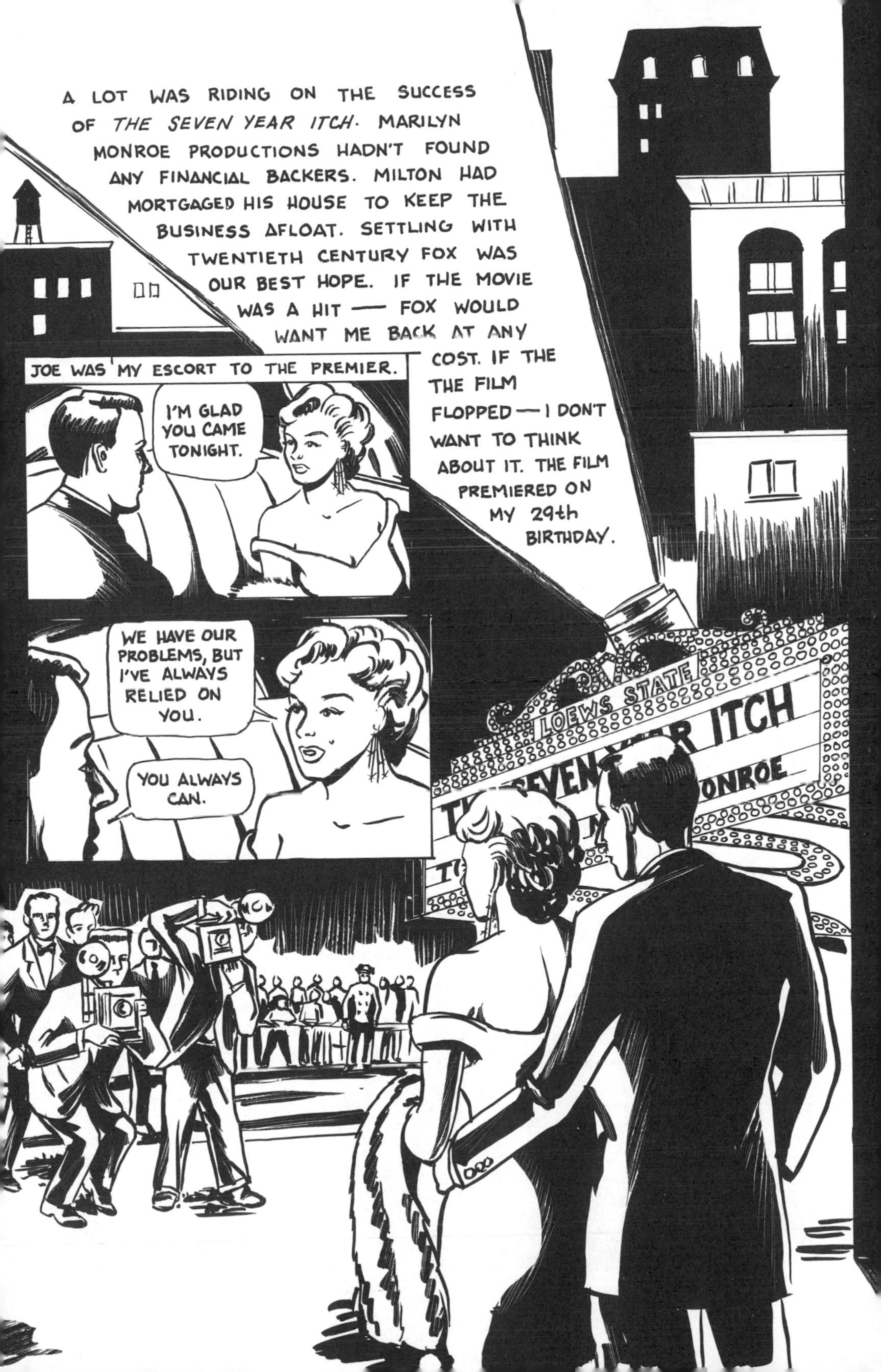

A LOT WAS RIDING ON THE SUCCESS OF THE SEVEN YEAR ITCH. MARILYN MONROE PRODUCTIONS HADN'T FOUND ANY FINANCIAL BACKERS. MILTON HAD MORTGAGED HIS HOUSE TO KEEP THE BUSINESS AFLOAT. SETTLING WITH TWENTIETH CENTURY FOX WAS OUR BEST HOPE. IF THE MOVIE WAS A HIT — FOX WOULD WANT ME BACK AT ANY COST. IF THE THE FILM FLOPPED — I DON'T WANT TO THINK ABOUT IT. THE FILM PREMIERED ON MY 29th BIRTHDAY.
JOE WAS MY ESCORT TO THE PREMIER.
I'M GLAD YOU CAME TONIGHT.
WE HAVE OUR PROBLEMS, BUT I'VE ALWAYS RELIED ON YOU.
YOU ALWAYS CAN.
LOEWS STATE
ITCH
ONROE

AFTER THE PREMIER

I THINK PEOPLE LIKED IT, DON'T YOU?

POLIO

WHERE ARE WE GOING?

JUST WAIT AND SEE.

HAPPY BIRTHDAY

SURPRISE!

LATER

MARILYN, ARE YOU AND JOE GETTING TOGETHER AGAIN?

NO, WE'RE GOOD FRIENDS.

DO YOU HAVE TO SAY IT SO FAST? AFTER ALL I'VE DONE.

I'M SORRY. THE PARTY'S WONDERFUL. YOU'VE BEEN WONDERFUL.

GOOD. THAT'S WHAT YOU SHOULD SAY.

SHOULD SAY?! NOBODY TELLS ME WHAT I SHOULD SAY!

NOT YOU AND NOT THOSE BASTARDS IN HOLLYWOOD!

I'M NOT GIVING UP. YOU'LL COME BACK.

MILTON HAD SET ME UP IN AN APARTMENT AT THE WALDORF ASTORIA. TRUE TO OUR PLAN, I WAS LIVING LIKE A MOVIE STAR. IT WAS LONELY.

I WISH ARTHUR WOULD CALL.

I GUESS HE'S BUSY WITH HIS NEW PLAY, HIS KIDS, ...HIS WIFE.

RING RING

HELLO!

OH, JOE.

NO, I'M NOT GOING TO CHANGE MY MIND... I DON'T HAVE TO TELL YOU WHY...!

MEN!

HE THINKS HE OWNS ME. HE THINKS WE'RE STILL MARRIED.

RING RING

JOE, IF YOU CALL ME AGAIN!

WHOOA! I'M INNOCENT! I HAVEN'T CALLED YOU IN YEARS.

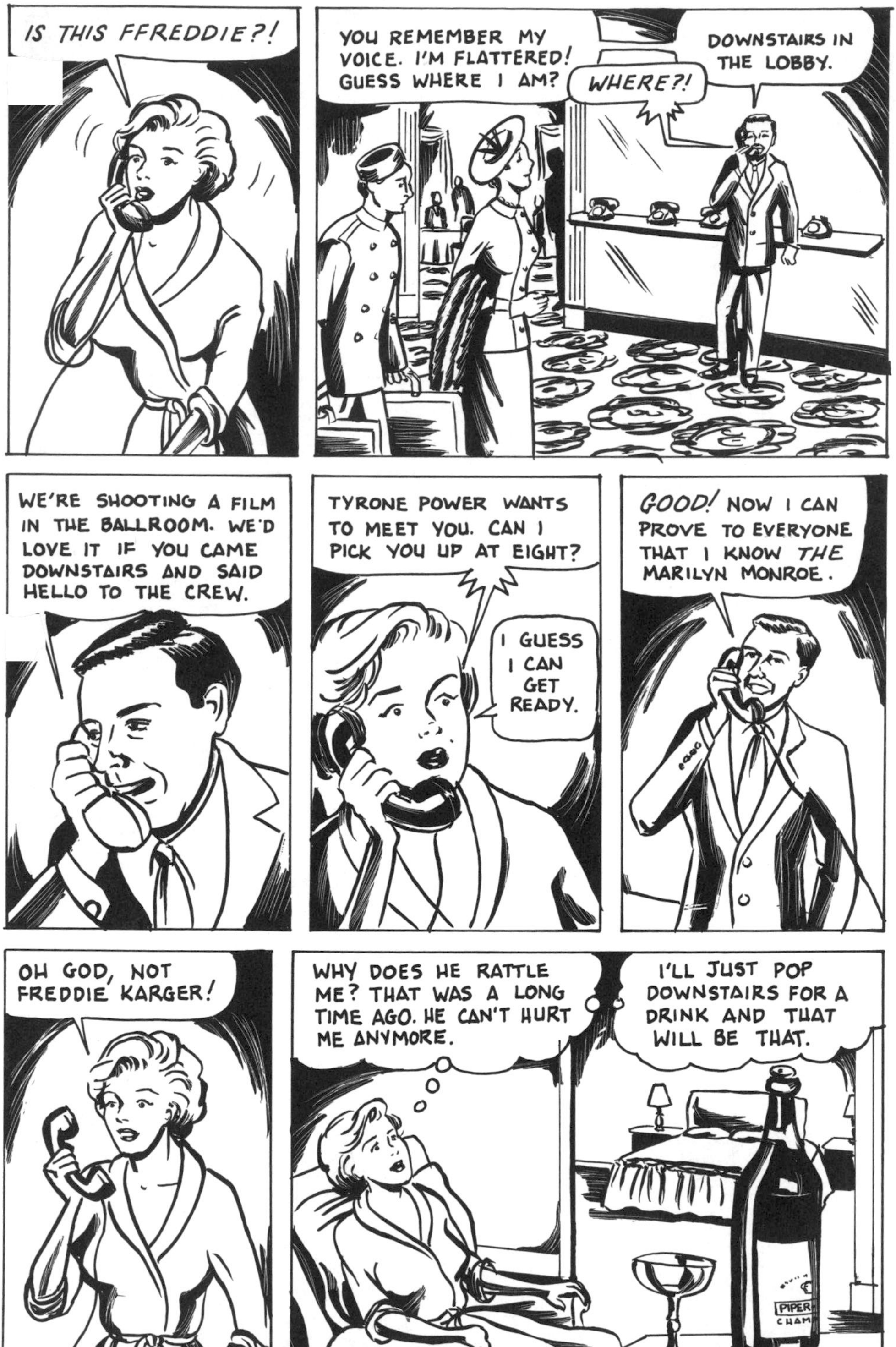
IS THIS FFREDDIE?!
YOU REMEMBER MY VOICE. I'M FLATTERED! GUESS WHERE I AM?
WHERE?!
DOWNSTAIRS IN THE LOBBY.
WE'RE SHOOTING A FILM IN THE BALLROOM. WE'D LOVE IT IF YOU CAME DOWNSTAIRS AND SAID HELLO TO THE CREW.
TYRONE POWER WANTS TO MEET YOU. CAN I PICK YOU UP AT EIGHT?
I GUESS I CAN GET READY.
GOOD! NOW I CAN PROVE TO EVERYONE THAT I KNOW THE MARILYN MONROE.
OH GOD, NOT FREDDIE KARGER!
WHY DOES HE RATTLE ME? THAT WAS A LONG TIME AGO. HE CAN'T HURT ME ANYMORE.
I'LL JUST POP DOWNSTAIRS FOR A DRINK AND THAT WILL BE THAT.
PIPER
CHAM

IF IT'S A MOVIE STAR THEY WANT, I'LL GIVE 'EM ONE.

TYRONE POWER WANTS TO MEET ME.

HA!

WHAT A HYPOCRITE.

HE NEVER WANTED TO KNOW ME WHEN WE WORKED TOGETHER ON THE FOX LOT.

HE'S ONE OF ZANUCK'S FRIENDS. HE'S PROBABLY A *SPY!*

ALL THOSE PEOPLE WHO ARE AGAINST ME... FREDDIE.

USED TO BE I WASN'T GOOD ENOUGH FOR HIM. NOW HE BRAGS HE KNOWS *MARILYN MONROE!*

I BET THAT ISN'T ALL HE BRAGS ABOUT EITHER.

MEN ARE SUCH BASTARDS!

I'M JUST THERE TO FILL THEIR NEEDS. NOT ONE EVER THOUGHT OF ME.

EXCEPT MAYBE JOHNNY, POOR JOHNNY... I'LL TELL YOU ONE THING THOUGH JOHNNY...

DING DONG

DREAMING ABOUT BECOMING A STAR WAS MORE FUN THAN BEING ONE.

DING DONG

WHAZHAT?!

DING DONG

MARILYN, WHAT TOOK YOU SO LONG?

OH FRED, I'M REALLY SORRY.

I JUST LOST TRACK OF TIME.

ARE YOU ALRIGHT?

YOU DON'T HAVE TO COME IF YOU'RE NOT UP TO IT.

NO, NO. I WANT TO.

YOU AND I OUGHT TO DRINK TO OLD TIMES. I'LL COME DOWN LATER, I PROMISE.

THE SEVEN YEAR ITCH WAS A BIG HIT. MILTON AND I GOT THE CONTRACT WE WANTED WITH SCRIPT AND DIRECTOR APPROVAL. AT LAST, I WAS ON THE THRESHOLD OF A NEW LIFE.

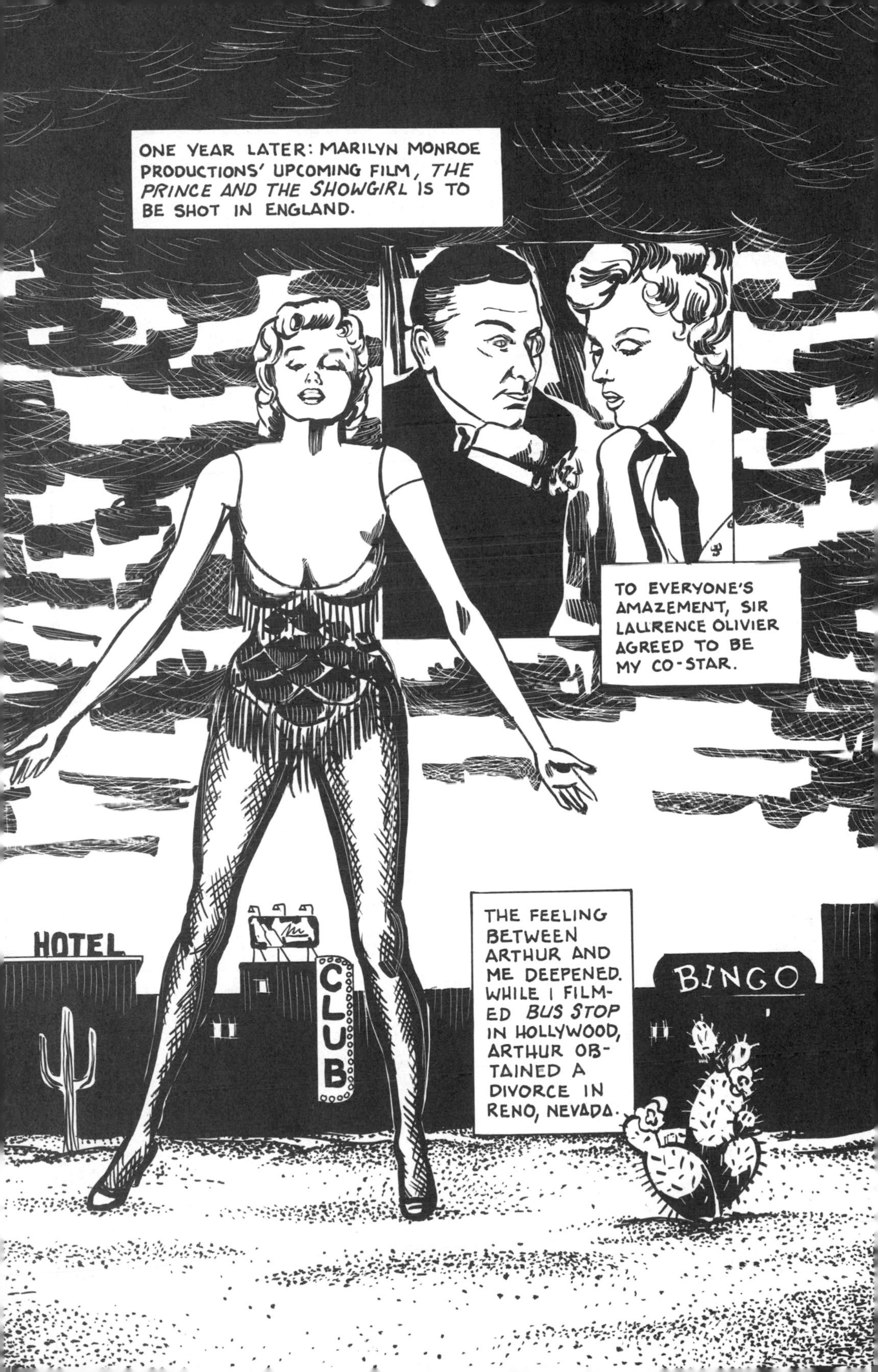
ONE YEAR LATER: MARILYN MONROE PRODUCTIONS' UPCOMING FILM, *THE PRINCE AND THE SHOWGIRL* IS TO BE SHOT IN ENGLAND.
TO EVERYONE'S AMAZEMENT, SIR LAURENCE OLIVIER AGREED TO BE MY CO-STAR.
HOTEL
CLUB
THE FEELING BETWEEN ARTHUR AND ME DEEPENED. WHILE I FILMED *BUS STOP* IN HOLLYWOOD, ARTHUR OBTAINED A DIVORCE IN RENO, NEVADA.
BINGO

WITH SUCCESS COMES PROBLEMS. I WAS USED TO CRITICISM, BUT NOT THE SORT MY ROMANCE WITH ARTHUR DREW.

AMERICA'S BEST KNOWN BLONDE MOVIE STAR IS NOW THE DARLING OF THE LEFT INTELLIGENTSIA, ONE OF WHOM IS HEADED FOR TROUBLE.

WALTER WINCHELL, RADIO AND NEWS- PAPER COMMENTATOR.

IS HE TALKING ABOUT US, ARTHUR?

THE HOUSE UNAMERICAN ACTIVITIES COMMITTEE WILL CHECK INTO HIS ENTIRE CIRCLE,

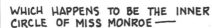

WHICH HAPPENS TO BE THE INNER CIRCLE OF MISS MONROE—

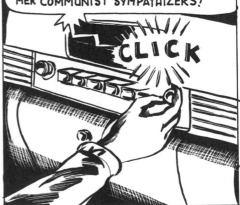

—AND ALL OF THEM ARE FOR- MER COMMUNIST SYMPATHIZERS!

CLICK

WHAT DID YOU EVER DO? GO TO A FEW MEETINGS AND SIGN A FEW PETITIONS.

YOU WERE NEVER A COMMUNIST!

THAT'S NOT THE POINT.

TYRANTS ALWAYS GO AFTER INTELLECTUALS AND ARTISTS. FREE THOUGHT IS MORE DANGEROUS THAN BULLETS.

I'M SORRY I GOT YOU INVOLVED.

DON'T BE SORRY. I'M PARTLY TO BLAME.

THEY WANT THE PUBLICITY OF 'MARILYN MONROE'.

IF IT WEREN'T FOR ME THEY'D LEAVE YOU ALONE.

THEY'VE BEEN WATCHING ME FOR YEARS. THEY'VE ALREADY REVOKED MY PASSPORT.

DON'T BLAME YOURSELF.

BUT I DID.

THE PRESIDENT OF 20th CENTURY FOX, SPYROS SKOURAS, PAID ARTHUR AND ME A PERSONAL VISIT AT MY APARTMENT.

ARE YOU IN LOVE, SWEETHEART?

YES.

WONDERFUL! YOU'RE A LUCKY MAN, ARTHUR. TAKE GOOD CARE OF HER, SHE'S LIKE A DAUGHTER TO ME!

I HOPE YOU'RE NOT GOING TO MAKE A MISTAKE WITH THE COMMITTEE.

I CAN ONLY DO WHAT'S RIGHT.

I *KNOW* THESE MEN.

THEY CAN BE REASON- ABLE. A PRIVATE SESSION CAN BE ARRANGED. *YOU UNDERSTAND?*

MR. SKOURAS, I CAN- NOT CO-OPERATE WITH THE COMMITTEE.

ARTHUR YOU HAVE MORE THAN YOURSELF TO THINK OF NOW. WHAT COULD THIS DO TO MARILYN'S CAREER?

I'VE TOLD ARTHUR NOT TO WORRY ABOUT ME. I WILL SUPPORT HIM WHATEVER HE DECIDES TO DO.

PEOPLE IN HOLLYWOOD ARE SUCH COWARDS.

WE WENT TO WASHINGTON SEPARATELY, TRYING TO AVOID THE PRESS. I WAITED AT THE HOME OF ARTHUR'S LAWYER, WHILE HE FACED THE COMMITTEE.

THE LIFE OF A WRITER IS PRETTY TOUGH. I'LL TELL YOU ABOUT MYSELF, BUT MY CONSCIENCE WILL NOT PERMIT ME TO USE THE NAME OF ANOTHER PERSON.

MORAL SCRUPLES DO NOT CONSTITUTE GROUNDS FOR REFUSING TO ANSWER A QUESTION.

WE CITE YOU IN CONTEMPT OF CONGRESS.

LATER THAT EVENING

WHAT DOES THAT MEAN? CONTEMPT OF CONGRESS?

WORST CASE SCENERIO, ARTHUR COULD GO TO JAIL FOR ONE YEAR.

JOSEPH RAUH, ARTHUR'S ATTORNEY.

DON'T WORRY, IT WON'T COME TO THAT.

RING RING

EXCUSE ME, WHILE I TAKE THIS.

ONE CONGRESSMAN ASKED WHY I WRITE SO TRAGICALLY ABOUT AMERICA?

THAT'S WHAT THIS IS REALLY ALL ABOUT. THEY WANT ME TO WRITE HAPPY, UPBEAT PLAYS.

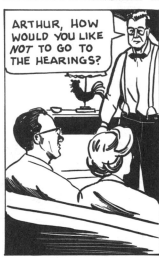

ARTHUR, HOW WOULD YOU LIKE *NOT* TO GO TO THE HEARINGS?

THAT WAS CONGRESS-MAN WALTERS* OFFICE. HE'S WILLING TO DROP THE WHOLE THING...

*WALTER WAS CHAIRMAN OF HUAC.

... IF MARILYN AGREES TO BE PHOTOGRAPHED SHAKING HIS HAND.

HA HA HA HA

OF COURSE, WE DECLINED.

I TRIED TO KEEP MY PRESENCE A SECRET, BUT THE PRESS FOUND ME.

DO YOU THINK MR. MILLER'S DIFFICULTY WILL AFFECT YOUR CAREER?

NO, I DON'T THINK SO.

WHAT DO YOU THINK THE OUTCOME OF THE HEARING WILL BE?

I BELIEVE WE WILL WIN.

ARTHUR HAD A PRESS CONFERENCE OF HIS OWN.

MR. MILLER, IS IT TRUE YOU'VE ASKED TO HAVE YOUR PASSPORT REISSUED?

YES.

I PLAN TO TRAVEL TO ENGLAND TO BE WITH THE WOMAN WHO WILL BE MY WIFE.

MR. MILLER DOES THIS MEAN YOU'RE MARRYING MARILYN?

I WILL MARRY MARILYN MONROE BEFORE SHE GOES TO LONDON TO MAKE A PICTURE.

WHEN SHE GOES TO LONDON, SHE WILL GO AS MRS. MILLER.

CAN YOU BELIEVE IT! HE JUST ANNOUNCED IT TO THE WHOLE WORLD!

YOU KNOW, HE NEVER REALLY ASKED ME.

THINGS TURNED OUT IN OUR FAVOR. ARTHUR GOT HIS PASSPORT. THE CONTEMPT OF CONGRESS CITATION WAS EVENTUALLY DROPPED.

ARTHUR MILLER AND MARILYN IN LONDON WITH LAURENCE OLIVIER AND VIVIAN LEIGH.

EVERYONE SEEMED TO THINK A MAN IN LOVE COULDN'T BE A COMMUNIST — ESPECIALLY IF HE WAS IN LOVE WITH "MARILYN MONROE."

NEW YORK CITY, 1958: MARILYN MONROE'S ATTEMPTS AT PERSONAL AND PROFESSIONAL FULFILLMENT ARE FALLING SHORT OF EXPECTATIONS. MARILYN'S PARTNERSHIP WITH MILTON GREENE HAS ENDED IN ACRIMONY AND HER MARRIAGE TO ARTHUR MILLER IS STRAINED. DESPONDENT OVER A MISCARRIAGE, RESTLESS AND SHORT OF MONEY, SHE'S READY TO GO...

BACK TO HOLLYWOOD

LEE STRASBERG'S APARTMENT

I HOPE I HAVEN'T MADE A MISTAKE!

I JUST TOLD BILLY WILDER THAT I'D DO ANOTHER MOVIE WITH HIM.

WHAT'S WRONG WITH THAT? I THOUGHT YOU LIKED BILLY WILDER.

I DO! IT'S JUST THIS ROLE. I CAN'T BELIEVE IN IT.

I PLAY THIS GIRL WHO'S SUPPOSED TO ACCEPT TWO MEN IN DRAG AS HER BEST GIRLFRIENDS.

HOW COULD SHE BELIEVE TONY CURTIS AND JACK LEMMON ARE GIRLS?

IT'S NOT SO DIFFICULT, REALLY.

THINK OF ALL YOUR PROBLEMS WITH WOMEN. THEY'RE JEALOUS OF YOU. YOU'VE NEVER REALLY HAD GIRLFRIENDS.

NOW SUDDENLY, YOU MEET TWO WOMEN WHO LIKE YOU, WHO WANT TO BE YOUR GIRLFRIENDS.

YOU'RE RIGHT! THAT'S RIGHT!

I ARRIVED IN HOLLYWOOD WITH PAULA STRASBERG, LEE'S WIFE, AS MY PERSONAL COACH.

I ALSO HAD MY PERSONAL MAKE-UP ARTIST, HAIR DRESSER, MASSEUR AND SECRETARY TO SUPPORT ME.

I MET MY CO-STARS, JACK LEMMON AND TONY CURTIS, WHO WERE BOTH WARM AND COMPLIMENTARY.

BILLY PERSUADED ME TO FILM IN BLACK AND WHITE BY SHOWING ME A TECHNICOLOR SCREEN TEST OF JACK AND TONY IN DRAG.

THEIR SKIN LOOKS GREEN!

BUT PROBLEMS ON THE SET OF *SOME LIKE IT HOT* BEGAN ALMOST FROM THE FIRST DAY.

WHAT'S TAKING SO LONG? I'VE BEEN WAITING ALMOST TWO HOURS.

DIRECTOR, BILLY WILDER

THIS EYEBROW IS WRONG. EVERYTHING MUST BE PERFECT BEFORE I FACE THE CAMERA.

MY CHARACTER, SUGAR KANE, IS A SINGER AND UKELELE PLAYER IN AN ALL GIRL BAND.

YOU STILL HAVEN'T GOT IT, DEAR.

IT'S NOTHING TO GET UPSET ABOUT. DON'T STRAIN FOR IT, DEAR.

I'M SORRY, I NEED PAULA.

I NEVER DO ANYTHING ON FILM I DON'T BELIEVE IN. EVERYTHING HAS TO COME FROM THE DEEPEST PART OF ME.

JESUS, IT'S BEEN HALF AN HOUR. BILLY'S REALLY STEAMED.

I'M READY NOW.

WHEN I WAS LITTLE, I EXPECTED TO BE PUNISHED FOR ABOUT ANYTHING.

THE FOSTER CHILD IS ALWAYS BLAMED AND SENT AWAY.

BEANSTALK!

I THOUGHT I MADE IT CLEAR, I DON'T WANT ANY DRINKING.

SWEET SUE, THE BAND LEADER.

JACK LEMMON AS DAPHNE.

WHEN I WAS LITTLE, I WAS ALWAYS AFRAID. I WAS SO GRATEFUL TO BE PROTECTED, TO HAVE A FRIEND.

THAT'S A WRAP!

DOES THAT MEAN I CAN TAKE OFF THESE SHOES?

PAULA, TELL ME THE TRUTH.

I WAS TERRIBLE, WASN'T I?

YOU WERE WONDERFUL, JUST WONDERFUL.

GOD HELP US.

THERE'S A NUT ON THE PLANE AND WE'RE IN MID-FLIGHT.

WHY DO YOU PUT UP WITH HER?

THIS GIRL MAY NEED A LOT MORE TAKES THAN YOU THINK NECESSARY, BUT WHEN SHE'S GOT IT RIGHT, IT'S WORTH IT.

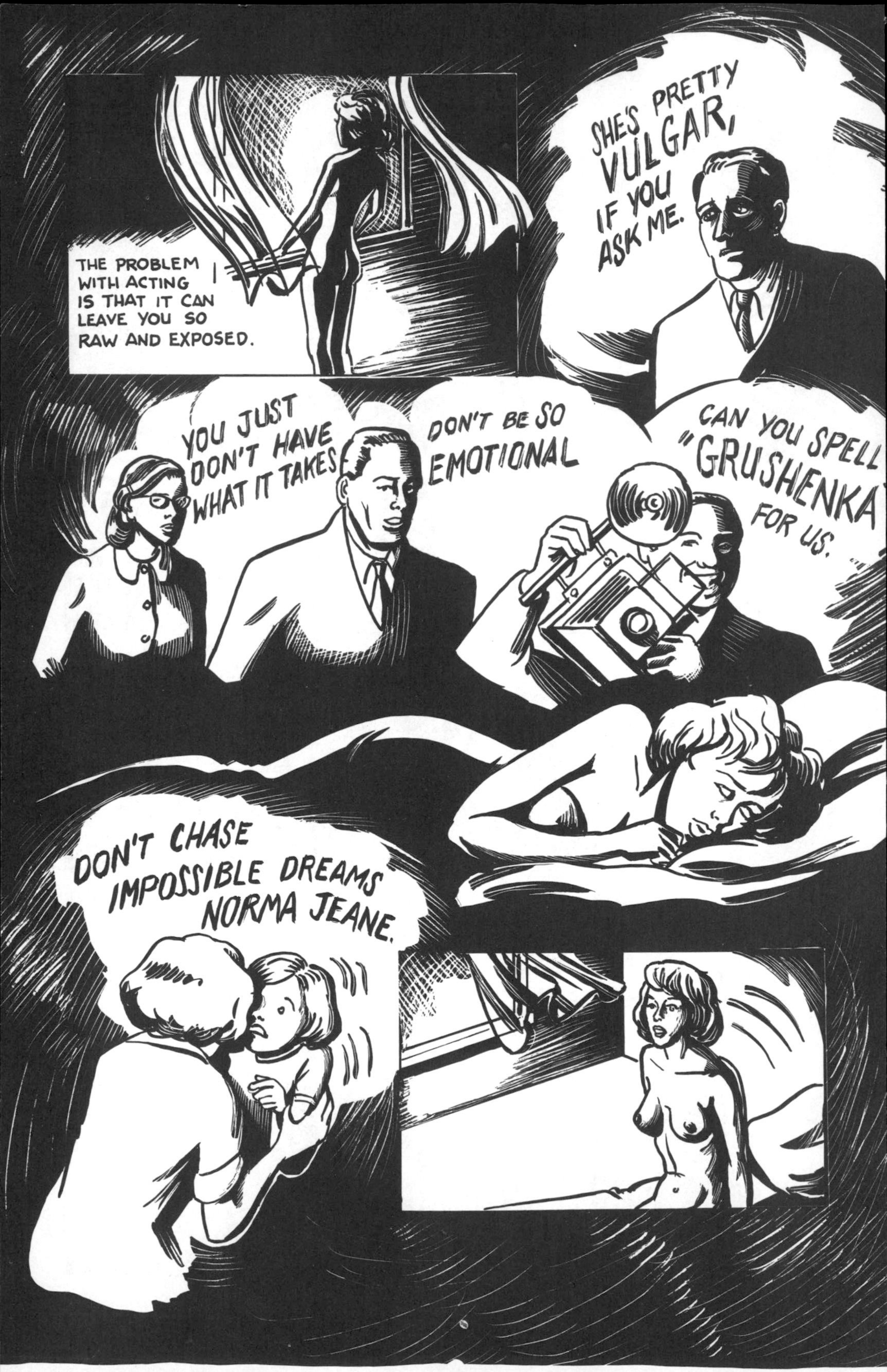
THE PROBLEM WITH ACTING IS THAT IT CAN LEAVE YOU SO RAW AND EXPOSED.
SHE'S PRETTY VULGAR, IF YOU ASK ME.
YOU JUST DON'T HAVE WHAT IT TAKES
DON'T BE SO EMOTIONAL
CAN YOU SPELL "GRUSHENKA" FOR US.
DON'T CHASE IMPOSSIBLE DREAMS NORMA JEANE.

I HAD TO MAKE THE RAWNESS GO AWAY, I HAD TO SLEEP.

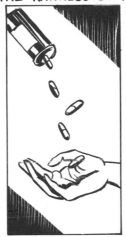

AAR-GGG

MARILYN?

PAULA WAS IN THE ADJOINING SUITE.

AAGAGG

OH GOD.

YOUR USE OF BARBITURATES WORRIES ME

I NEED THEM TO SLEEP.

MY GYNECOLOGIST, DR. KROHN

IF YOU WERE PREGNANT, ONE COULD BRING ON A MIS-CARRIAGE.

I COULD GIVE IT UP, IF I WERE PREGNANT.

MORE THAN BED REST, I NEEDED A PROTECTOR, LIKE SUGAR NEEDED DAPHNE.

HELLO, ARTHUR.

ARTHUR ARRIVED WHILE WE WERE ON LOCATION.

MY CONFIDENCE ON SET IMPROVED, AT FIRST.

IT'S AMAZING WE NEVER RAN INTO EACH OTHER BEFORE.

I'M SURE I WOULD HAVE REMEMBERED ANY-ONE AS ATTRACTIVE AS YOU.

YOU'RE VERY KIND.

TONY CURTIS AS 'JUNIOR'.

I BET YOU'RE ALSO GENTLE AND HELPLESS.

I BEG YOUR PARDON?

YOU SEE, I HAVE THIS THEORY ABOUT MEN WHO WEAR GLASSES.

WHAT THEORY?

I'LL TELL YOU WHEN I GET TO KNOW YOU BETTER.

CUT!

AND THAT'S A TAKE!

THREE PAGES OF DIALOGUE IN ONLY ONE TAKE. AMAZING!

I WAS FEELING MUCH BETTER. ARTHUR WAS WITH ME AND I WAS PREGNANT AGAIN.

THE FRESH AIR AND SUN WILL BE GOOD FOR THE BABY.

AT OTHER TIMES, I COULDN'T IGNORE THE HOSTILITY.

HOW MANY TAKES DO YOU THINK SHE'LL NEED TODAY?

15 TAKES?

I SMELL A 30 TAKER COMING ON.

JACK LEMMON AS 'DAPHNE'

TONY CURTIS AS 'JOSEPHINE'

$50?

IT'S A BET.

TAKE 3

ACTION.

WHAT'S THE MATTER, SUGAR?

WHERE'S THE WHISKEY?

CUT!

MARILYN DARLING, YOUR LINE IS "WHERE'S THE BOURBON?"

TAKE 9.

SCENE 141

TAKE 9

SOME LIKE IT HOT

WILDER 9-2-58

WHERE'S THE BOTTLE?

TAKE 21

WHERE'S THE BABY?

SCENE 141 TAKE 21
SOME LIKE IT HOT
WILDER 9-2-58

TAKE 46

WHERE'S THE BON-BON?

SCENE 141 TAKE 46
SOME LIKE IT HOT
WILDER 9-2-58

LOOK MARILYN, WE'VE WRITTEN IT DOWN.

SO WHEN YOU OPEN UP THE DRAWER, JUST READ THE LINE.

THIS BROAD CAN'T EVEN LEARN ONE LINE.

AT TIMES LIKE THIS, I TURNED TO PAULA.

YOU'RE A VERY SENSITIVE ARTIST. IT'S THE HOSTILITY THAT'S UPSETTING YOUR CONCENTRATION.

BILLY'S A GOOD MECHANICAL DIRECTOR, BUT HE'S NOT SUBTLE. WE HAVE TO MAKE SUGAR KANE OUT OF NOTHING.

SHUT OUT ALL DISTRACTIONS. REACH DOWN AND FIND SUGAR KANE IN YOURSELF.

MOST OF ALL, EVEN MORE THAN PAULA, I NEEDED MY HUSBAND.

I SHOULD BE DOING REAL ACTING, LIKE *ANNA CHRISTIE,* NOT SUGAR KANE.

YOU WERE THERE, YOU SAW HOW THEY TREAT ME!

MARILYN, YOU'LL NEVER HAVE THE RESPECT OF YOUR PEERS IF YOU BEHAVE UNPROFESSIONALLY.

I EMBARRASS YOU, DON'T I?

I DIDN'T SAY THAT.

I CAME HERE TO SUPPORT YOU, I DEFEND YOU.

YOU MEAN YOU MAKE EXCUSES FOR ME.

ARTHUR, YOU DON'T THINK I'M A GOOD ACTRESS.

MARILYN, YOU HAVE TO BELIEVE IN YOURSELF, FIRST OF ALL.

BUT YOU BELIEVE IN ME, DON'T YOU?

YES, I BELIEVE IN YOU.

BUT I FELT HE WAS JUDGING ME.

I TRY TO MELD MYSELF TO MY CHARACTER, TO MAKE HER REAL.

HAVE YOU EVER TRIED AMERICAN GIRLS?

WHY?

ANYTHING?

THANKS, JUST THE SAME.

YOU SHOULD SEE A DOCTOR, A GOOD DOCTOR!

CUT!

AND THAT'S A TAKE.

WELL, I DON'T FEEL RIGHT ABOUT IT.

I'M SORRY, I HAVE TO DO IT AGAIN.

WELL MARILYN, MAYBE IF YOU TRIED...

DON'T TALK TO ME NOW, I'LL FORGET HOW TO PLAY IT.

WHAT ABOUT ME? IF I EAT ANYMORE OF THIS I'LL TURN INTO A CHICKEN.

I WASN'T THERE THE NIGHT THEY SCREENED THE RUSHES OF MY SCENE WITH TONY. PAULA TOLD ME WHAT HAPPENED THAT NIGHT.

TONY, WHAT'S IT LIKE KISSING MARILYN MONROE?

KISSING HER IS LIKE KISSING HITLER.

TONY, HOW COULD YOU SAY THAT?

PAULA, YOU TRY ACTING WITH HER.

SEE HOW YOU LIKE IT?

MARILYN MONROE ~ TONY CURTIS JACK LEMMON

BILLY WILDER ——.."SOME LIKE IT HOT"

SOME LIKE IT HOT WAS A HUGE SUCCESS.

SEEING THE FILM YOU'D NEVER GUESS WHAT MAKING IT WAS LIKE.

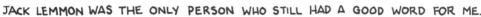

JACK LEMMON WAS THE ONLY PERSON WHO STILL HAD A GOOD WORD FOR ME.

IN THE SUMMER OF 1962 MARILYN MONROE WAS FIGHTING TO SAVE HER REPUTATION AND CAREER.

HER LAST TWO FILMS HAD BEEN DISAPPOINTMENTS AT THE BOX OFFICE. AFTER BOUTS WITH DRUGS AND ILLNESS, MARILYN WAS FIRED FROM THE FILM *SOMETHING'S GOT TO GIVE.* HER STUDIO PUBLICLY CRITICIZED HER FOR "FLOUTING PROFESSIONAL DISCIPLINE."

THAT LAST SUMMER MARILYN MONROE WAS BUSY POSING FOR PHOTOGRAPHERS, PUTTING OUT HER SIDE OF THE STORY THROUGH A SERIES OF INTERVIEWS.

THE LOST INTERVIEW

6

PERHAPS YOU'D LIKE SOME REFRESHMENTS WHILE YOU WAIT.

HOW DO I LOOK? DO I LOOK ALRIGHT?

YOU LOOK STUNNING.

I GUESS I DON'T LOOK BAD FOR AN OLD BROAD OF 36.

ARE YOU SURE I LOOK ALRIGHT?

DON'T WORRY, YOU'LL HAVE THEM EATING OUT OF YOUR HANDS.

HELLO. I'M SORRY I KEPT YOU WAITING.

HELLO MISS MONROE, I'M ANN MORTON AND THIS IS JOE BERG, MY PHOTOGRAPHER.

PLEASE, CALL ME MARILYN.

HOW DO YOU LIKE MY HOUSE? DID YOU LOOK AROUND? THIS IS MY FIRST HOUSE.

I OWNED A FARM WITH MR. MILLER, BUT THIS HOUSE IS ALL MINE.

I'M STILL FURNISHING IT.

A LOT OF PEOPLE WOULD HAVE EXPECTED A BIGGER HOUSE, SOMETHING MORE GLAMOROUS.

THIS ISN'T A MOVIE STAR'S HOUSE.

OH, BUT I LIKE THAT. IT'S MORE REAL.

NONE OF MY NEIGHBORS ARE ACTORS OR IN THE BUSINESS. JUST PEOPLE.

I DO HAVE A SWIMMING POOL, SO IT'S A LITTLE LIKE A STAR'S HOUSE.

THE INTERVIEW BEGINS

I REMEMBER THE FIRST TIME I SAW MY NAME IN LIGHTS.

GASP!

IT FELT VERY EXCITING AND STRANGE.

I HOPE SOMEONE SEES IT.

MAYBE SOMEONE I KNEW IN HIGHSCHOOL WILL DRIVE BY.

BUT I GUESS NONE OF THEM KNOW THAT NORMA JEANE IS "MARILYN MONROE".

THEN I FELT KINDA SAD.

BACK IN THOSE DAYS I USED TO PASS BETTY GRABLE'S DRESSING ROOM DOOR. SHE WAS THE BIGGEST STAR ON THE LOT. I WAS IN AWE OF HER.

MAYBE I'LL HAVE A DRESSING ROOM LIKE THAT SOMEDAY.

A YEAR LATER I WAS THRILLED WHEN THE STUDIO ARRANGED AN INTRODUCTION.

WAIT A MINUTE.

LET'S GET A PICTURE OF YOU FIRST.

NOW STAND BY THE DOOR AND LOOK SEXY.

?!

Betty Gra

THEN I REALIZED THAT THIS WAS THEIR WAY OF TELLING MISS GRABLE I WAS GOING TO BE HER SUCCESSOR.

HEY, WHERE DO YOU THINK YOU'RE GOING?

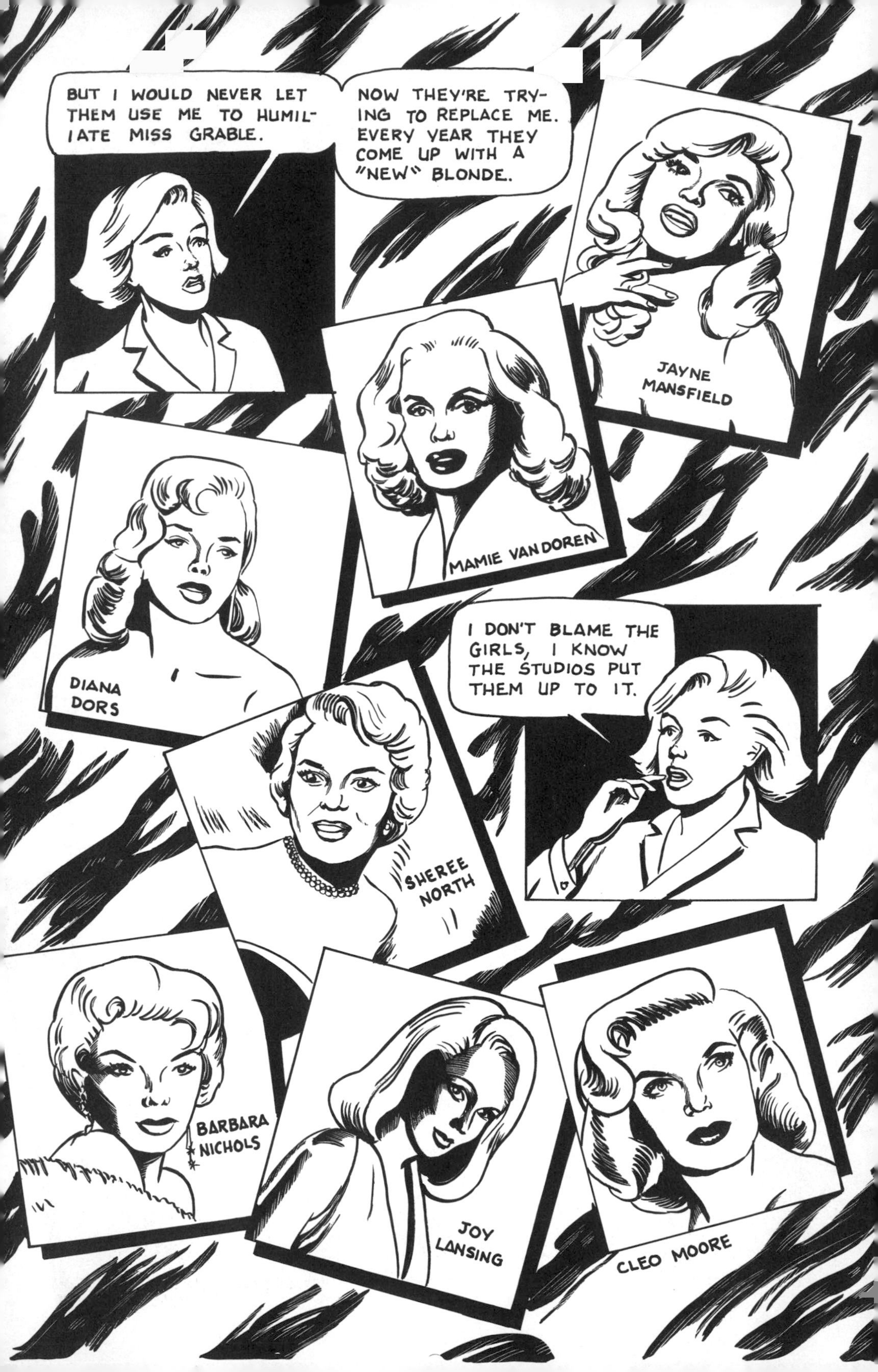
BUT I WOULD NEVER LET THEM USE ME TO HUMILIATE MISS GRABLE.
NOW THEY'RE TRYING TO REPLACE ME. EVERY YEAR THEY COME UP WITH A "NEW" BLONDE.
JAYNE MANSFIELD
MAMIE VAN DOREN
DIANA DORS
I DON'T BLAME THE GIRLS, I KNOW THE STUDIOS PUT THEM UP TO IT.
SHEREE NORTH
BARBARA NICHOLS
JOY LANSING
CLEO MOORE

In Hollywood they think blondes are a dime a dozen.

After they fired me from this last film, they moved Lee Remick in the next day.

Only Dean Martin — my co-star — walked out. "No Marilyn—no film", he said. I was really pleased.

'SOMETHING' STALL BEGINS TO PALL

Nothing gave again yesterday in 20th-Fox's 'Something's Got To Give' dilemma. Today marks the second week of layoffs for cast and crew of 104. Despite intense efforts by

Star's Illness Poses Problem

Studio in Crisis on Marilyn Monroe

Hints of drastic studio action were heard today because of Marilyn Monroe continued absence from Century Fox picture,

'Something' (Someone) Will Have to Give Now

All parties concerned in 20th-Fox's "Something's Got to Give" yesterday wouldn't.

Producer Henry T. Weinstein asserted, "The picture is stalled and we don't know when it will be resumed." He referred all quest-

MM ABSENCE GIVES 20th 'SOMETHING' TO WORRY ABOUT

Marilyn Monroe's failure to appear yesterday on the 20th-Fox lot for the second day in a row, had executives reportly reappraising entire 'Something's Got To Give' situation within the next few days.

20th-Fox Reported Finally Dropping Monroe from 'Give'

Although official confirmation was not forth coming from the studio, it was reliably learned yesterday that 20th-Fox has dropped MM from 'Something Has Got to Give'.

20th-Fox To Replace Ill Monroe

A spokesman for 20th Century Fox said today the studio has contacted Kim Novak "and every other actress in and out of town" to replace MM in her latest picture.

I USED TO LOVE TO PLAY WHEN I WAS LITTLE. THEN I LEARNED THIS WAS "ACTING". I LIKE THE CREATIVE PART OF ACTING.

ON THE SET OF *SOMETHING'S GOT TO GIVE* WITH DIRECTOR GEORGE CUKOR.

MARILYN, MEET YOUR "CHILDREN," CHRIS AND ALEXANDRA.

WE'RE GOING TO HAVE A LOT OF FUN ON THIS FILM, I PROMISE.

ONLY THINGS GET BETWEEN YOU AND ACTING. SOMETIMES YOU SEE HUMAN NATURE AT ITS VERY WORST.

IF MY BABY HAD LIVED, SHE WOULD HAVE BEEN THE SAME AGE AS THAT LITTLE GIRL.

WHY WOULD THEY CAST THAT WOMAN AS A MOTHER?

IF THEY SEE YOU'RE VULNERABLE, THEN THEY GO IN FOR THE KILL.

EVERYONE KNOWS SHE'S THE BIGGEST WHORE IN THE WORLD.

IN THIS SCENE, YOU SEE YOUR CHILDREN FOR THE FIRST TIME IN FIVE YEARS.

PLACES.

I GAVE UP ON HOLLYWOOD EXECUTIVES LONG AGO, BUT THE PEOPLE ALWAYS ACCEPTED ME, ALWAYS LIKED ME.

WHEN THEY SEE ME UP ON THE SCREEN, THEY KNOW IF I'M BEING HONEST.

IT'S THE PEOPLE WHO MADE ME A STAR.

DOES MY PRESS SECRETARY HAVE YOUR PHONE NUMBER?

I MAY HAVE SOME GOOD NEWS, SOON.

OH?!

CAN YOU GIVE ME A CLUE? I'D LIKE TO USE IT, BUT I HAVE A DEADLINE.

SORRY.

I CAN ONLY TELL YOU IT'S WORTH WAITING FOR.

THAT'S WHAT SHE SAID, "SOMETHING WORTH WAITING FOR."

WHAT DO YOU THINK?

I THINK SHE'D DO ANYTHING TO SAVE HER CAREER. I ALSO THINK THE PUBLIC CAN'T GET ENOUGH OF HER.

RIGHT

CALL HER IN A FEW DAYS. SOFTEN HER UP. SHE MIGHT CONFIDE IN A WOMAN.

A FEW DAY'S LATER

YES, I'M AWARE OF WHAT SHE SAID, I'M HER PRESS SECRETARY.

WELL, CAN I TALK TO HER?

MISS MONROE HAS NO STATEMENT AT THIS TIME.

CLICK!

ON A HUNCH, I DROVE TO HER STREET AND WAITED.

MAY I SIT DOWN?

YOU!

I'M INTRUDING, I KNOW, BUT YOUR SECRETARY WOULDN'T PUT MY CALLS THROUGH.

SHE'S JUST DOING HER JOB.

ARE YOU ANGRY?

I SUPPOSE YOU'RE JUST DOING YOUR JOB. IF I WERE A REPORTER I'D BE THE SAME WAY.

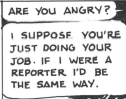

I LIKE TO COME HERE AND WATCH.

I WANTED TO HAVE A CHILD I GUESS I WAITED TOO LONG.

WELL, MAYBE I WOULDN'T HAVE BEEN A GOOD MOTHER.

YOU LEARN THOSE THINGS WHEN YOU'RE YOUNG. I NEVER HAD A NORMAL LIFE, NORMAL EXPERIENCES.

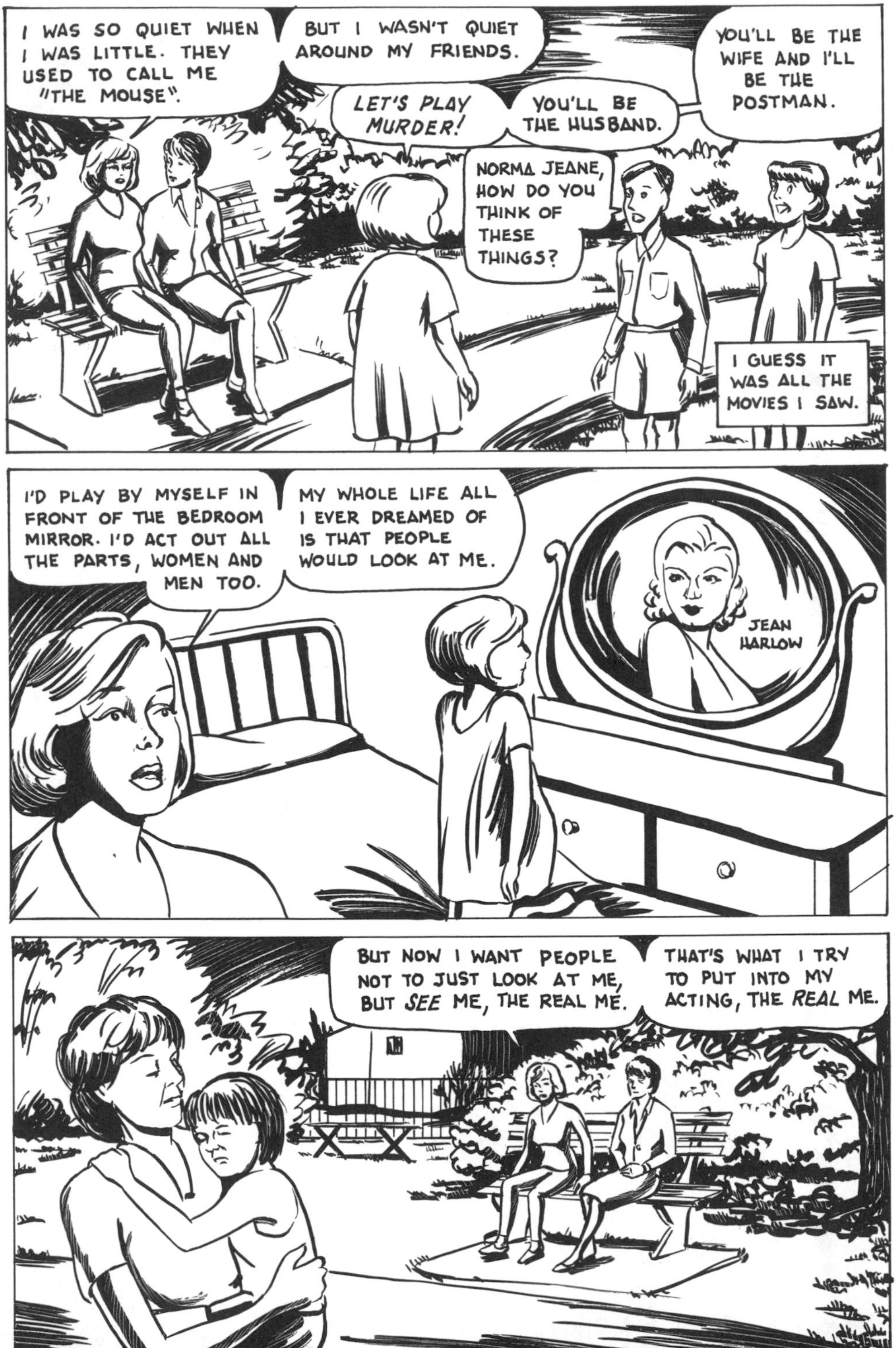
I WAS SO QUIET WHEN I WAS LITTLE. THEY USED TO CALL ME "THE MOUSE".
BUT I WASN'T QUIET AROUND MY FRIENDS.
LET'S PLAY MURDER!
YOU'LL BE THE HUSBAND.
YOU'LL BE THE WIFE AND I'LL BE THE POSTMAN.
NORMA JEANE, HOW DO YOU THINK OF THESE THINGS?
I GUESS IT WAS ALL THE MOVIES I SAW.
I'D PLAY BY MYSELF IN FRONT OF THE BEDROOM MIRROR. I'D ACT OUT ALL THE PARTS, WOMEN AND MEN TOO.
MY WHOLE LIFE ALL I EVER DREAMED OF IS THAT PEOPLE WOULD LOOK AT ME.
JEAN HARLOW
BUT NOW I WANT PEOPLE NOT TO JUST LOOK AT ME, BUT SEE ME, THE REAL ME.
THAT'S WHAT I TRY TO PUT INTO MY ACTING, THE REAL ME.

MY MARRIAGE TO MR. MILLER BEGAN TO FALL APART AFTER THAT LAST MISCARRIAGE.

BUT I'LL NEVER SPEAK HARSHLY OF ANY OF MY HUSBANDS — I KNOW YOU REPORTERS WOULD LIKE IT IF I DID.

MEN AND WOMEN HURT EACH OTHER — BUT NOT BECAUSE THEY WANT TO.

DO YOU THINK THOSE PEOPLE ARE HAPPY?

I LIKE TO THINK THEY ARE.

I DON'T BELIEVE ANYONE'S HAPPY ALL THE TIME. EVERYONE HAS THEIR PROBLEMS.

MAYBE YOU'RE RIGHT, MAYBE I EXPECT TOO MUCH.

STILL, I WOULD LIKE TO BELIEVE IN THE POSSIBILITY OF HAPPINESS.

IF YOU WEREN'T A WOMAN, I'D SAY YOU MUST HAVE SLEPT WITH HER.

WE'VE DECIDED TO DO A PHOTO SPREAD WITH CAPTIONS BASED ON YOUR INTERVIEW.

YOU'RE RIPPING THE GUTS OUT OF MY PIECE!

DON'T WORRY, YOU'LL GET PAID.

YOU MADE HER SEEM TOO SYMPATHETIC! I THOUGHT YOU WERE ONTO SOMETHING JUICY.

DIDN'T YOU CALL HER?

YES, BUT SHE HAD NO STATEMENT.

I DON'T KNOW WHY I SAID THAT. MAYBE I DIDN'T WANT TO HEAR ANYMORE ABOUT HOW SOFT I AM.

MAYBE I FELT PROTECTIVE OF HER.

EVENTUALLY TWENTIETH CENTURY FOX REHIRED MARILYN TO FINISH *SOMETHING'S GOT TO GIVE.* THEN—IN LESS THAN A WEEK—MARILYN WAS DEAD.

NEWSWORLD

Woman's Journal

MARILYN'S LAST PHOTOGRA[

SEE

TIME PASSES. MARILYN'S NOT FORGOTTEN— FAR FROM IT. EVERY YEAR THERE'S ANOTHER BOOK, ANOTHER FILM CLAIMING TO EXPOSE THE "REAL MARILYN."

Children's Corner

WHO KILLED MARILYN?

NO SCHOOL TODAY

LIL' PUPPY

I MET MARILYN BRIEFLY, I DON'T CLAIM TO HAVE KNOWN HER.

GRANDMA!

I THOUGHT I SAW SOME SPARK.

LOOK WHAT I HAVE FOR YOU.

I STILL SEE IT FROM TIME TO TIME...

WILL YOU READ TO ME?

I'LL READ IT AT BEDTIME.

...IN THE FACES OF SMALL CHILDREN.

AND THEY LIVED HAPPILY EVER AFTER.

GOODNIGHT, HONEY.

I LOVE YOU, GRANDMA.

AFTERWORD

I was standing in my kitchen making toast and thinking about shopping for school clothes, when the news of Marilyn Monroe's suicide came over the radio. That moment, exactly where I stood, the August morning light, are fixed in my memory like a polaroid shot. I was shocked. How could anyone so alive be dead? It hardly mattered that I had never met the woman. By the time I was twelve, Marilyn Monroe already had a grip on my imagination.

As I was growing up, I would rediscover Marilyn Monroe every few years. I eagerly consumed each revived film, discovered photograph, and new book. Marilyn seemed to grow in depth and complexity as I did. When I became an artist, a woman artist at that, my empathy for Marilyn grew. I became dissatisfied with the way she was portrayed in the media. The glitzy, artificial icon, the simpering self-destructing addict, the sexual adventuress, the victim of a dozen different conspiracy theories—all distort, oversimplify, and deprive her of her humanity. "My" Marilyn was flawed, funny, brave, troubled, but, most of all, hard to pin down. I appreciate that about Marilyn. She frustrates all attempts to have the final say, to own her. In life Marilyn fought all attempts to categorize her, to limit her. She still insists on being her own person.

This is a fictionalized biography of Marilyn Monroe, based on my research and imagination. My methods are not unlike film biographies, which use composite characters, condensation of time, and educated guesses. In Chapter One, I imagine Marilyn telling the story of her childhood in a psychiatric session. It is true that Marilyn Monroe was a patient of psychiatrist Dr. M. Kris, as are the facts of her childhood presented here, but what was actually said in those sessions is sealed. In Chapter Two, there is a scene where Marilyn visits a graveyard. A number of people have asked me if this is something I imagined. It is a story Marilyn told to her husband, Arthur Miller. He apparently believed it and published it in his autobiography. That's good enough for me. In Chapter Four, Marilyn meets with a studio executive and lays out her complaints about how her contract limited her choice of roles. This probably never occurred as a one-on-one meeting, but was carried out between lawyers over a period of months. For dramatic purposes and for the sake of readers' attention spans, the incident is reduced to a one-page confrontation. Chapter Six, "The Lost Interview," was based in part on an interview Marilyn gave to the French magazine MARIE CLAIRE and an interview and photo session she gave to LIFE magazine that was published a few days before her death. The woman interviewer was based on Flora Rheta Schreiber whose interview for GOOD HOUSEKEEPING magazine was killed for being too sympathetic. As for Marilyn's "voice," I built my dialogue from existing interviews and my own sense of how Marilyn would speak.

Researching this book, I read everything that I could find currently in print on Marilyn Monroe. Some of my primary sources were LEGEND by Fred Lawrence Guiles, MY STORY by Marilyn Monroe, MARILYN MONROE by Donald Spoto, GODDESS by Anthony Summers, THE UNABRIDGED MARILYN: HER LIFE FROM A TO Z by Randall Riese and Neal Hitchens and Arthur Miller's autobiography, TIMEBENDS. There are a wealth of photo surveys devoted to Marilyn Monroe. Some of the ones I most relied on were MARILYN AMONG FRIENDS by Sam Shaw, MONROE by James Spada, and MARILYN AT TWENTIETH CENTURY FOX by Lawrence Crown. Many hours were spent at the New York Public Library, both at the picture collection and the Billy Rose collection, which supplied photo material for my drawings of automobiles, movie houses, street cars, fashions, the Empress Josephine, and more.

There are a number of people whose help I gratefully acknowledge: Suzanne Ball, Ann Decker, Howard Kogan, Peter Kuper, Seth Tobocman, and my editor and publisher, Dan Simon, who took a chance on me.